P9-AOF-298

Contents

Preface and Acknowledgments

I was inundated with clients with eating disorders around 1987. At that time women in the midwest had limited information about these problems. I wanted to write something that would help women understand the issues they faced relating to food, weight, and dieting. Women needed to know that there was hope for recovery—that they could look forward to resuming full and rewarding lives after dealing with their eating disorders. And I wanted to place the blame for these culturally induced illnesses where I felt it belonged: on the image makers in our culture who promote the notion that we women are not slim enough.

Although *Hunger Pains* sold well locally, it was soon out of print, and I moved on to other projects. However, I've continued to receive requests for this book for the last eight years. I think this continued interest in *Hunger Pains* has two causes. First, the book offers insights about our culture's effect on women's relationships to their bodies. Second, women everywhere are still suffering from eating disorders. In fact, the main change over the last 10 years has been that girls are getting eating disorders at even younger ages. At this point, even fifth and sixth graders are turning up as clients.

I'm pleased Adams Publishing is reissuing *Hunger Pains*. This edition is hopefully just as readable as the original, but I have updated the statistics, added new examples, and expanded the discussion of eating disorders in children. I have also added suggestions designed to help women who want to work on their own food-related issues, as well as a new chapter on the need for cultural change.

One of the problems in writing this book is deciding how to refer to heavy women. The word "fat" is loaded with negative connotations. "Overweight" commonly refers to large, but not obese women. The term implies that we somehow know the ideal weight for that particular woman. "Obese" is properly clinical, but generally refers to only the largest of women. Where to divide the two groups is subjective. Most researchers give a pound or percentage limit. I have used the words *heavy*, *large*, or *overweight* to describe women who weigh more than most women. When I use the word *obese*, it refers to women who cannot fit into standard clothing.

You will find references throughout the book to "junk food." I use the term to describe food that is high in sugar, salt, fats, or oils. Junk food has packaging that is probably more expensive than the food itself. It tends to be heavily advertised and cleverly marketed. This is not the kind of food health-conscious parents would want their children to eat on a regular basis.

Readers may be less familiar with the term *lookism*. I use it to mean the stereotyping of individuals on the basis of their appearance. To be "lookist" is to pay attention only to appearances and to make many assumptions about another's character, behavior, and worthiness based on that appearance.

We should also deal with the ambiguity of the word *diet*. One of the word's meanings is, simply, what we eat. It can also mean a prescribed regimen for losing weight. This kind of "diet" has two critical aspects: external means are used to control eating, and its goal is weight loss. For example, many dieters follow programs that list exact menus for every day of a given time period. The dieter hopes that using the menus to control her caloric intake will help her lose weight. I vehemently oppose this kind of diet.

Coming out against diets does not mean abandoning an emphasis on good nutrition. On the contrary, the next to last chapter of this book recommends developing healthy eating habits. I also recommend that the way we control our eating be internal, rather than external. We can learn to respect our own food preferences and listen to the messages we get from our stomachs. The importance of internal control is discussed in the chapter on hunger and eating.

The challenges we face are complicated by the role advertising plays in determining our eating habits, and by the way we use food in cultural rituals such as holidays and celebrations. Many people are hooked on junk foods, and may well be addicted to sugar. For a time, it may be tough to answer questions like, "Do I really want to eat?" and "What do I want to eat?" But asking ourselves these questions can help us establish new patterns. I can not promise that changing one's behavior around issues of hunger and eating is easy. I can only suggest that it is possible—and that it leads to healthier and happier women.

Eating disorders were a terrible tragedy in 1987, as they still are today. I wrote *Hunger Pains* in the hope that it would help women everywhere examine their relationships to their own bodies. I also hope the book spurs women to further examine the noxious role that mass culture plays in the development of girls and women. We can work together to change the culture to make it more positive and supportive for women.

All of the clients described in this book are composite characters. I have changed any identifying characteristics so that no client will have his or her confidence betrayed by the text. Similarities between real people and my characters may exist because women with eating disorders often wrestle with similar problems; however, all such likenesses are accidental.

There are many people to thank for their help with *Hunger Pains*, starting with all of the clients who shared their problems with me. Also, I'm grateful to Jim for his advice and encouragement, to Sara for her research, and to Zeke for coming up with a title. I appreciate the love and support of all my aunts—Henrietta Isbell, Grace Teague, Betty Robinson, Agnes Loutzenhiser and Margaret Nemoede. I thank all of the Brays, Pages and Piphers, especially Bernard and Phyllis Pipher who are always there for me. I thank my agent Susan Lee Cohen who has been my friend through thick and thin times and my editors Jane Isay and Joelle Delbourgo. Jerry and Dani Weinberg, Catherine Kidwell, Ivy Ruckman, Carolyn Johnsen, Kent Haruf, and John DeFrain all gave me advice. Sherri Hanigan, Jan Zegers, Ginger Haruf, Jan Stenberg, Dee Byrd, Wenda Miller, Laura Wertz, and John Lehnhoff read the manuscript and offered suggestions. Thanks also to Sue Zajic, Reynold Peterson, and Tom Hansen for help with the initial publishing. Thanks to the Prairie Trout—Marge Saiser, Pam Barger, Twyla Hansen, and Karen Shoemaker—for their unfailing support and guidance. Thanks finally to my current editor, Ed Walters, for his help with this new edition.

CHAPTER ONE

Overview

On a recent plane trip, a stunningly beautiful woman slid past me to take the window seat. I noted her slim body, finely manicured nails, and designer clothes. She carried a leather briefcase and notes about a shoot in Chicago and a photo session in Los Angeles.

During the flight I concentrated on my writing while she read a novel. When the meal was served I happened to glance her way. I was stunned to see she was eating her turkey, rice, and salad with her hands. I quickly looked away, then back to make sure I'd seen what I thought I had seen. She was shoveling her food into her mouth like an animal. Why would such a beautiful woman eat this way?

I imagined that she must have a severe eating disorder. Perhaps she only ate (or binged) when she was alone, and had forgotten that most people eat with silverware. When the model finished her food, she excused herself to use the restroom. When she returned, I noticed the telltale scar running along her index finger. This scar had formed from repeatedly sticking her hand down her throat to induce vomiting. It was no accident that the most beautiful woman I had seen on my trip of several weeks had a raging eating disorder.

I wrote *Hunger Pains* because, as I listened to my clients talk of their feelings about their bodies, as I worked with women with eating disorders, and as I spent time among my female friends, I realized that something terrible was happening. Women all around me were rejecting their bodies and loathing what was most basic, their own flesh. In loathing their flesh, they loathed their personhood. As my client Cassandra said so eloquently, "In this society you have to be pretty first, then you can think about having character, being smart, and achieving things. If you aren't pretty, nothing else matters."

A hundred conversations with friends and clients had triggered my concerns. However, the impetus to act came when my caseload filled with women with eating disorders. Before the mid-1980s, I had had no experience with women with these problems. In all my years as a graduate student in psychology, I had never interviewed a woman with an eating disorder. Then, all of a sudden, every other caller was a woman with one. There was an epidemic raging in our community and we had no vaccination or cure.

Clients had anorexia or bulimia and were food- and weight-obsessed. Anorexic women were starving themselves to the point of severe emaciation. Bulimic women binged on enormous amounts of food and then vomited or used laxatives to avoid weight gain. As I lectured on eating disorders, I was struck by how much intensity food issues generated in women. A television reporter asked me if I knew that Jane Fonda was "guilty of bulimia." After the show, some people in the studio approached me to say, "Bulimia sounds disgusting." Others came quietly and said, "I've got a problem with that. Can you help me?" For weeks after the show, the office phone was busy with women calling for help. I was flooded with requests to speak, give workshops, and consult with diet support groups. Counselors at our three local universities all called to discuss the problems they faced with female students. Bulimia was a significant problem in our community and treatment resources were minimal.

The professional literature suggested that the incidence rate for bulimia among college-age women was as high as 25 percent. Until I actually experienced masses of women coming to me for help, I had been relatively indifferent to the numbers. Now I was alarmed.

I began thinking more about women and weight. As I reviewed my practice of many years, my first insight was that I had yet to encounter a woman who liked and accepted her own body. Women of all sizes and shapes, including a model and an ex-Playboy bunny, hated their bodies. They saw at least some part as gross or flabby. Women as skinny as chopsticks tried to convince me that they had jiggly behinds or pot bellies. Lovely college women insisted they had double chins or fat thighs.

While it is possible that women in therapy are more likely to misperceive and criticize their bodies, recent psychological research indicates that virtually all women are ashamed of what they consider inferior bodies. Women also distort their body images—90 percent of all women overestimate their own body size. Women are preoccupied with their weight. Who among us has not heard a tiny woman say when offered dessert, "No thanks, I'm dieting," or "I shouldn't—I've put on so much weight recently." Who do you know who likes to try on swimsuits or thinks she looks all right in a bikini?

Most of my female friends, both traditional and feminist, share a common disdain for their bodies. Most try to control their eating and consider themselves fat. Recently, my friend Sandra came over for an evening of conversation. We sat in front of a fire on the last snowy night of the winter with a bottle of red wine, sharp cheddar cheese, crackers, and pears. We talked about politics, art, and books. Sandra is a great talker with the capacity for incisive analysis and sparkling wit. But every time she had a slice of cheddar, she interrupted her conversation to comment, "This will be my last" or "I feel evil tonight." Sandra was not an exception. Like most of us, she'd been socialized to apologize for her appetites. Food was her enemy. Her body was her enemy. To enjoy food was to sin.

Another friend, Cecilia, appears sophisticated, assertive, and confident. But she isn't. She is terrified that she will lose her husband as she grows older and her stomach gets rounder. She diets compulsively and every week she sees a therapist who hypnotizes her and suggests she feel no hunger. When we go out for lunch, Cecilia orders a small salad with lemon juice and talks longingly of chocolate bars and pasta.

I am angered by the needless suffering of all these women. Even more powerful, though, than my anger is my concern for the future. I have an eight-year-old niece who swims and plays basketball. Like most girls her age, Fay is fond of unicorns, Ramona books, and kittens. She plays the violin and piano and loves rock and roll. She's big, the tallest person in her class, and probably the heaviest. She'll be over six feet tall someday, muscular and large-boned. I don't want her to suffer the way women of my generation, and even the girls of my son's generation, suffer. She knows she is beautiful now and is proud of her strength and size. I cannot bear the thought of her affection for her body being eroded by television, rock videos, and ads. I don't want her to grow up judging herself by impossibly harsh and narrow standards. Fay is proud and confident and I want her to stay that way.

We are living in a culture that promotes a monolithic, relentless ideal of beauty that is quite literally just short of starvation for most women. "You can't be too rich or too thin." For so many of us, thinness equals attraction, which equals value. This formula has created a generation of women whose behavior is self-destructive and whose thinking about themselves is punishing.

We are pelted with messages that our bodies need to be smaller, leaner, and more shapely. Bookstores carry shelves of diet books. One Saturday at our grocery store, my daughter Sara and I counted 56 articles on slimming down advertised on magazine covers. Diet camps, exercise spas, diet support clubs, and the low calorie industry flourish. Billions of dollars are going to those who can simultaneously trigger our fears and promise help.

I remember a magazine cover, "Karen Carpenter Dies of Anorexia Nervosa—A Rare Mental Disease." In her final photograph she was emaciated, rickety, and her muscles had atrophied to the point she could barely walk or hold up her head. In the same magazine, on the very next page, was a rum ad with a picture of a model in a white bikini. She was stretched out in a sexually provocative way, but she looked a lot like Carpenter.

To be a woman is to have a body image problem. For women, harmful eating patterns are becoming the norm. Women diagnosed as bulimic or anorexic are merely the extremes on a universal continuum.

Women's alienation from their bodies has a tremendous personal and social cost. Eating disorders are tragic problems, sometimes fatal, but more often involving years of pain and unhappiness. My clients' obsessions with food and critical feelings about their bodies affect every aspect of their lives, from moods to work performance to the ability to form and maintain intimate personal relationships.

The cause of these disorders does not lie primarily within

individual women. Rather, the pathology is in our media and wherever else the image of an ideal female body is propagated. As I am writing this, I think of the current issue of *Sports Illustrated*, which shouts at me from the shelves of every airport bookstore, neighborhood market, and magazine stand in America. The annual swimsuit edition displays a thin but buxom model on the cover. Her body is not one found in the natural world. It makes me angry that, even as I treat women with eating disorders, our culture creates more propaganda like this to encourage self-starvation.

Every day, 56 percent of the women in the United States are on diets. We have a 30-billion-dollar-a-year diet industry. Slender junior high school girls skip lunch to lose weight. Many young smokers are afraid to stop for fear they'll gain weight. High school girls reject birth control pills because they could cause them to gain a few pounds. Better to risk a pregnancy!

To treat eating disorders in America is to treat our culture. We need a revolution in our values and behavior. We need to define attractiveness with much broader parameters, so that most women, not an infinitesimal few, can feel good about their appearance. We need to emphasize other characteristics—industry, integrity, talent, intelligence, and good humor—in evaluating the worth of women. Until our culture changes the messages it sends about women it will be difficult for individual women to have healthy attitudes about their bodies.

Every day at work I listen to young women who have lost sight of all goals except to control their weight. I hear math students and flute players obsess about their backsides. I consider whether the young women I see need to be hospitalized for health reasons. I've grown tired of treating the casualties of this lethal cultural attitude.

As a nation, we don't have the resources to treat all the damaged psyches of women who hate their bodies. Prevention, rather than treatment, needs to be our primary goal. If we can change the way we raise our children, the way our media portrays women, and the attitudes we have toward our bodies, my work treating our culture's victims will become unnecessary. The energy, time, and money that women now waste worrying about their weight can be put to better use. Our daughters will grow up strong, healthy, and proud. Together we will have won an important victory.

CHAPTER TWO

The Link Between Hunger and Eating

Most of us can think of personal stories that demonstrate the strong link between food and emotions. A friend of mine who is the daughter of Lebanese immigrants told me about her humiliation when she was a Girl Scout. When the troop came to her home, her mother served baklava. My friend desperately wanted to belong to American culture and have the right things to eat like Fritos and Kool-Aid.

Another friend, Barbara, told me that when she was five, her mother served her a large helping of broccoli and insisted she eat it. Barbara hated broccoli and refused. After many unsuccessful verbal threats, her mother force-fed her the broccoli, which she immediately threw up. Her mother, enraged by Barbara's refusal to keep the food down, forced her to eat her broccoli vomit. To this day, Barbara gags at the thought of broccoli.

The language of eating is rich in metaphor, and words associated with food and hunger have strong emotional connotations. Phrases like "eat him alive," "gobble him up," "hungry for your love," "starving for affection," "the milk of human kindness," "we're cooking now," and "food for thought," are but a few examples. Fairy tales often feature food. Rapunzel, for example, was given to a wicked witch at birth because her father was caught stealing spinach from the witch's garden to feed his pregnant wife. The price the couple paid for their greed was the loss of their only child.

Perhaps the most vivid of all food stories is Hansel and Gretel, in which two children are rejected by their stepmother and left in the woods to starve. A house of gingerbread lures them to the wicked cannibal witch. The children are almost food themselves before they escape. In this old story the association between the hatred of the stepmother and food withdrawal is absolute.

Food is also closely associated with love, nurturing, and giving. My favorite restaurant, the Soul Food Kitchen, serves great jambalaya. I once asked the cook for her secret and she winked at me and said, "There's a little love in every bite."

As I write about the meaning of food and eating, I'm struck by how they connect with everything—power, love, families, sex, punishments, rewards, rejection, and euphoria. Primal and powerful, our hunger and eating behaviors are related to our most basic views of ourselves and our fellow humans.

Our ways of eating are intimately connected with the rest of our lives. Women who have lost control of their eating have lost control of their lives. I think of all the women who feel badly about themselves because of their bodies, of women who could be growing and developing, but instead are controlled by their obsessions with their weight. If these women can regain control of their eating, many other parts of their lives will become manageable as well.

Natural Hunger

Our bodies send us many cues that keep us alive and healthy. For example, when we swim underwater, our lungs begin to tighten and ache as our need for oxygen grows. They send us an urgent message—we need to breathe. Internal cues from our bodies send us important messages regarding sleep, temperature control, and pain. We ignore these cues from our body at great peril to our health. Hunger is an internal cue from our body telling us that we need nourishment. Hunger pangs are a survival tool; after a certain point starving people no longer feel hunger. When this happens, they are close to death.

Newborn babies cry when they feel hungry, and cry increasingly more loudly until they are fed. For an infant, the need for food is painful, immediate, and all-absorbing. Good parents will respond quickly and feed their children. Infants will eat till they are satiated and then stop. Once full and relaxed, babies sleep or play. As babies grow older, other needs become salient, for example, the needs to explore and communicate. As their stomachs grow larger they can eat and store more food. By the time they are toddlers, children can even be stalled a bit when they are hungry.

Hunger, like most instincts, must be socialized. Just as we train children where to urinate and sleep, so we train them to use certain tools to eat at certain places and certain times. We don't eat lasagna for breakfast or serve hot dogs at banquets. Some foods are unacceptable to certain cultures. Muslim cultures prohibit the eating of pork and traditional Jewish homes do not serve meat and milk together. Americans do not eat insects, whereas in some cultures insects are a dietary staple. Some foods are eaten to celebrate holidays, such as turkey on Thanksgiving or cake on birthdays.

Eating becomes both a social and a survival behavior. We develop very civilized ways of meeting our primitive needs. At dinner time, a famished Victorian gentleman would not walk into a garden, pull up some carrots, shake off the dirt, and eat them raw. Rather, he'd have his manservant make reservations at his club. He would dress carefully, ride to the club, and only after he'd had a cocktail would he order a hearty meal.

In our culture children learn that they have some choices. Babies have food preferences and are quite capable of spitting out whatever mom or dad spoons in. Older children often have rigid eating patterns. I remember a two year old who visited us. Jane was going through a phase when she would eat only peanut butter sandwiches. For an entire week that's all she ate, in spite of her parents' embarrassed coaxing that she try other foods.

At one time families had an easier time developing healthy eating habits. Children ate primarily home-grown foods. Physical labor and walking kept most people at healthy weights. But over the last 40 years, two developments have made it harder to maintain a healthy relationship between the hunger instinct and eating behaviors. We have the mass marketing of sugary, non-nutritious foods and an increasingly sedentary population. Most adults do sedentary labor and many children and adults spend hours in front of the television. A recent study showed a high correlation between the number of hours of television watched and obesity in children.

Advertisers bombard children with messages to buy syrup-coated cereals, candy bars, and soda pop. These foods are linked with fun, family, fame, and love. Much to Sara's delight, I paid her to watch Saturday-morning TV and record the number of junk food commercials. In a three-hour period, she counted 32 food commercials. None of the foods advertised was nutritious. The ads promised strength, popularity, or agility if the child would only eat the product advertised.

Our old cultural adage, "It's as easy as taking candy from a baby," could well be changed to, "It's as easy as selling candy to a baby." Children are vulnerable consumers who like bright packaging and trust smiling, attractive adults who urge them to buy. Grocers place candy and gum right by the check-out stand so children will have plenty of time to look over the treats as their parents wait in line. Good parents will constantly struggle with their children about food. If they say no, their children will beg, wheedle, or pout, hoping their parents will give in. Either way, everyone loses.

Recently I was in a grocery store early in the morning. A father who'd worked a night shift was buying bacon and eggs. His little daughter, barely awake, snuggled happily into her dad's chest. As he paid, the clerk pulled out a stale sack of Christmas candy that the store was "giving away" to children. She pressed it on the father who said shyly, "No, thanks. We try to keep her from eating too much candy. It spoils her meals." Meanwhile the little girl began to cry, and what had been a happy time turned grim and tense.

One year our scruples got the better of us and we decided to give Halloween trick-or-treaters bananas and oranges. Our own children were mortified by our rudeness and warned their friends not to come by. The little ghosts and goblins that did stop looked none too happy with such healthy snacks. Another friend told me of a year when they were out on Halloween. They left an enormous tray of apples on their porch for the trick-or-treaters. When they returned home, the apples were untouched.

Psychologists design behavioral control systems using candy as rewards. Friends and family are only slightly less systematic. Children who behave badly are often denied the desserts or treats that good children receive as rewards. Unhealthy foods seem especially likely to be used as rewards. Some dentists even give lollipops as rewards for having no cavities. Few parents would dare to say, "You've done such a good job at school today that I'll give you some celery."

Social Eating

Eating is probably our most ancient form of social activity. Millions of years ago, we humans sat together around a fire and ate shared meals. Many of the stories in the Bible tell of feasting and working together to prepare food. Today in our culture many families report that the only time they are together is at dinner. When friends are together, food and drink are often the social cement.

The flip side of the social quality of eating is that mealtime can be very painful for lonely people. Many single adults have poor eating habits because it isn't fun to eat alone. Widows talk of the sadness of eating by themselves. A recently widowed client told me, "Until you're alone, you don't realize how much of a meal is talking. Now that I'm by myself, eating feels so primitive." A jewelry saleswoman said to me, "I can order whatever I want on the road. I have an expense account. But I do not enjoy a lobster dinner by myself. When I eat alone, I lose my appetite."

Eating produces a natural sedation. Digestion activates the parasympathetic nervous system. This branch of the autonomic nervous system returns the body to normal after it has responded to stress. Following a stressful situation, the parasympathetic system signals the heart to resume beating at its slower, normal rate. It relays messages for muscles to relax. Breathing slows down and pupils contract. The parasympathetic system is at work when we are deeply relaxed—after orgasm, just before falling asleep—or after a meal.

As a result, we generally feel better after we eat. In addition to the action of the parasympathetic system, there are certain foods that are especially calming. Milk contains a natural sedative that encourages drowsiness and sleep, which is why a glass of warm milk helps fight insomnia. Babies generally nap after their meals. Most of us have experienced the marked sedative effects of heavy eating. Remember the nap attack after a big business lunch? Think of how you feel after a holiday meal. Good hosts know that to encourage conversation, it is important not to serve too much food.

People under stress often rely on the sedative quality of food. Eating can be used to deaden a pervasive sense of loss or failure. Think of our custom of taking foods to homes when there is a death in the family. Here in the midwest, funerals are often followed by rich sit-down lunches. Food can quell anxiety and take the edge off panic.

In general, eating can be used to avoid dealing with negative feelings. But the painful feelings inevitably recur because the source of the pain has not been examined. Like alcohol, food can provide only a temporary escape. Women, especially, are experts at eating when hurt or angry. We swallow our anger. We kill our emotional pain with sugar.

Paradoxically, eating can also be a way of expressing feelings. It can be a way of saying "I hate you" or "I hate myself." I think of a chubby teenager who eats a bag of sweets that her parents have forbidden. Rejecting food can also be used to punish the person offering the food. For example, a client of mine was married to a man who had many affairs. He was a gourmet cook who loved to feed his wife elegant meals. Alice would not eat those fine meals. Dangerously thin, she hovered around 90 pounds and would only nibble at the dinners her husband begged her to enjoy.

Some women try to lose weight in organized programs. Some are bribed by their husbands or parents. Others compete with friends and coworkers. For some women, to be on a diet is to feel superior to those "slobs" who are chubby. When women are dieting, they often feel optimistic about their future as a thin person. Dieting does not lead to thinness, but it may cause temporary weight loss.

Not eating gives some women the illusion of being in control of their lives. Feelings are messy and painful. One way to reduce the complexity of the emotional world is to reduce reality to one dimension. If one is losing weight, life is under control. Judy Mazel, author of the Beverly Hills diet, advised, "Make your scale your best friend and lover." Sadly, many women have done just that. Never mind the bad job, the punishing relationship, the nuclear weapons build-up, or the destruction of the ozone layer. They are on a diet. Whether or not it's a good day depends on what the bathroom scales have to say.

Internal Versus External Control

Eating is an extraordinarily complicated biological, social, and psychological process, but people make decisions about eating in two fundamentally different ways. One is by relying on one's own internal cues or messages about hunger and satiety. This method requires awareness of how one's stomach feels and is called internal control. The external method relies on external cues such as ads, dieting advice, the smell of popcorn in a movie theater, or pizza on a street corner. A woman who walks by an ice cream store and decides to go in for a double dip even though she really isn't hungry is relying on external control for her eating decisions. All of us rely on external cues to a certain extent. We eat at mealtimes with our families even if we aren't terribly hungry, or we take a piece of gum when it's offered by a friend. It is only when we rely almost entirely on external cues that we run into trouble.

We have some evidence that externally controlled eaters are more likely to be obese than internally controlled eaters. Their eating habits are more easily manipulated than are those of internally controlled eaters. That does not mean that all obese or overweight people depend on external control. But it does suggest that an average woman will gain weight if she goes from being an internally controlled to an externally controlled eater. A woman without internal control of her eating is more vulnerable to the constant barrage of commercials and food ads. Like a sailboat with no centerboard, she is vulnerable to whatever forces blow her way.

Externally controlled eaters grow fat when food cues are abundant. And in our society, food cues are everywhere. Sara extended her studies of television to evening hours and recorded 43 food commercials in a three-hour period. Suffice it to say, most of the commercials were for high-calorie, high-fat food. But the commercials were artfully concocted and geared toward making viewers want to eat. For example, one ad showed a picture of a delicious-looking hamburger for several seconds. Then the ad asked, "Aren't you hungry now?"

The market place has encouraged women to abandon themselves to using external cues to determine when and how they eat. Women are more easily manipulated that way, and there is money to be made in manipulating women's eating. The junk food industry and its twin, the diet industry, both profit from our impulse eating and subsequent guilt and shame.

At a most basic level a diet is a form of externally controlled eating. It says, "Use me, not your stomach, to make decisions about eating." Diets turn people away from internal control and contribute to obesity by encouraging internally controlled eaters to become externally controlled. Once a dieter has learned to ignore her own cues, she becomes more vulnerable to the whole spectrum of external messages about food, not just those found in her diet books.

One diet book author reassured women, "Don't worry. After 18 hours of no solid food, you usually lose your hunger pangs and the acute desire to eat." Hunger should be cherished and respected just as the impulse to breathe is cherished and respected. If it works, we should stop fixing it.

Suggestions for Dealing with Hunger

1. Nutritious foods can be just as tempting as junk food. Keep delicious, satisfying snack foods available, so that your eating is healthier.

2. When you are tempted to eat, take a moment to think about your feelings. Are you really hungry, or are you tired, restless, angry, or lonely?

3. Once you have identified your feeling, deal with it directly and appropriately. If you are tired, take a nap. If you are restless, find something interesting to do. If you are hungry, eat.

4. Eat slowly and enjoy the sensations of eating.

5. Avoid using food as a means of avoiding other issues in your life. If you are in a problematic relationship, or unhappy or anxious about life, make understanding and dealing with these issues a top priority.

6. Exercise daily. Choose exercise that is fun and enjoyable. Participate in physical activities such as taking a walk or canoeing with friends.

7. Pay greater attention to your internal cues. Learn to use hunger and satiety to regulate your eating.

8. Do not eat to be polite or to avoid wasting food. Don't be a member of the clean plate club.

9. Develop ways to reward yourself that don't involve food. Watch a sunset, feed the geese at a nearby lake, or read a book.

10. Find other ways besides food to reward children. Take them to the library, go for a bike ride, or play a game of cards with them. Adult attention is the best reward of all.

CHAPTER THREE

What We See in the Mirror

> "I feel pretty, oh, so pretty. I feel pretty and witty
> and free."
> MARIA, IN *WEST SIDE STORY*

> "I'm so ugly and fat that I want to stay in my
> apartment all the time. I'm an eyesore. People look
> at me and think that I'm disgusting and should kill
> myself."
> CASSANDRA, IN THERAPY

Men and women talk about their bodies in very different ways. In all my years as a therapist, I have never seen a male client whose appearance was his primary concern. Even single men experiencing rejection are unlikely to blame their problems on their appearance. When I ask male clients how they feel about their bodies, most are surprised by the question. They will pause for a minute and then say something like, "Fine, I guess. I never really thought about it." If they have complaints, they tend to be complaints related to performance. For example, "I'm not much of a jock" or "I've got a little arthritis that keeps me off the golf course."

Generally, men describe their appearance with more accuracy and detachment. Tony, for example, was a good-looking young factory worker who came into therapy after a painful rejection by a lover. When I asked about his appearance, he said, "I know I'm good-looking. I always have been. So what? Looks aren't what matters in the long run." Claude, a short, balding accountant, told me, "I'm no prize winner in the looks department. But I can get along with anybody and that's what counts."

This is not to say that men have no body image problems. Obese men and short men often feel physically inadequate. Also, men as a group are becoming less satisfied with their bodies. A survey published in *Psychology Today* reported that in 1972, only 15 percent of men said they were unhappy with their appearance. By 1986, 54 percent of all men were unhappy with their appearance. Increasingly, men feel the same pressures that women feel to be attractive and slender. If these trends continue, the incidence rate for eating disorders among men will increase.

However, this book will not deal with men's problems. That is not to minimize their problems, only to suggest that men's problems are outside the scope of my expertise. As a therapist, my work on body image has been primarily with women. Also, at the present time, women's problems are much more common. The ratio of women to men with eating disorders is 50 to 1.

Research has shown that men tend to evaluate their bodies realistically and their self-appraisals match up with the appraisals of others. Women behave differently. As a group, women consistently see themselves as fatter and less attractive than others see them. Many come in with laundry lists of complaints about their bodies. Women will talk with chagrin about a tiny mole on their arm or eyelashes that are stubby.

A friend of mine who worked in a clothing store told me of another interesting difference between the sexes. She said, "When men try on clothes, they talk about the clothes. When women try on clothes, they talk about how awful their bodies look in the clothes."

Most commonly women bemoan their fat. They hate fat and blame themselves for what they consider a repulsive flaw. Many relate long and painful histories of diets, surgeries, and other suffering caused by their weight.

My experience as a therapist is that very plain women and beautiful women suffer the most from "lookism," our society's tendency to judge women based on their appearance. Beautiful women are often in therapy for self-esteem problems. Because they have always been valued for their attractiveness, they have no faith in their own internal qualities. Also, they are afraid others will discover they are not really that beautiful. Especially as they grow older, beautiful women are afraid of losing the one quality that makes them acceptable: their appearance.

Very plain women, on the other hand, may have some confidence in their skills and talents, but they are not asked out and are in therapy because they are lonely and rejected. Moderately attractive women are the luckiest. They participate in social situations and are valued for other dimensions besides their appearance. They are more likely to attribute their social successes to their personalities or characters.

Why is it that women are so damaged when it comes to body image? Why are we so vulnerable in this area? Why do most of us feel like such failures? One critical factor is the messages we receive as children about our bodies.

From the first years of life, children hear comments about their bodies. Girls hear remarks about their attractiveness. "She's as pretty as a picture" or "She's going to be a real looker." Boys hear remarks related to the instrumentality of their bodies. "If he keeps growing this way, he'll be a basketball star for sure" or "He's a muscular kid. He'll be great on the football team." These comments are internalized and form the basis of a child's developing self-image. By the time children reach kindergarten, they can describe themselves physically. Most girls think they are cute and that being cute is pretty important. Most boys think they are strong and athletic.

In the elementary school years, both girls and boys enjoy the experience of their bodies growing and becoming stronger and more competent. For both sexes, the emphasis is on function. Most children take pride in being fast runners or good athletes. Even at this age, though, the messages that girls receive about athletics are more complex. They are encouraged within limits. Some girls report they have been warned against becoming too muscular because it's not attractive. They are warned against beating boys if they want to be popular. They are teased about being a tomboy if they are too interested in sports. Even the most successful girls in athletics experience boys' sports getting more coverage and money than theirs do.

Boys know that the skills they learn regarding sports will be valued in junior high and high school. Until recently, girls were expected to stop sports at puberty and devote themselves to looking attractive. Who cared if a 15-year-old girl was great at hurdle jumping? Fortunately, this may be changing with the new interest in women's athletics.

Early adolescence is a critical time for the formation of body image. While adolescents are painfully eager to please the opposite sex, their bodies are changing into new adult shapes. This is the era of acne, greasy hair, training bras, and feet as big as boats. Young teens spend hours in front of the mirror examining their bodies for flaws, bulges, and curves. My niece April, when she was 14, was prone to putting on elaborate makeup and combing and recombing her hair. I would tell her that other things besides looks are important. April would say, "Not at my school."

Boys are lucky because many factors influence their body image. Boys evaluate their bodies in terms of strength, speed, and agility. They value bodies as instrumental in winning trophies, fending off bullies, and working for good wages. Girls, such as April, tend to zero in on only one aspect of their bodies—their attractiveness.

There is another sex difference at this age. During puberty, girls' bodies grow softer, rounder, and broader. Before puberty, girls have 10 to 15 percent more fat cells than boys. After puberty, they have twice as many. Thus, just at the time when girls are desperate to be slim, their fat tissue increases. The natural process of development is working against what most girls want. Boys, on the other hand, want to be taller, more muscular, and stronger. Time is on their side.

Early adolescence seems a particularly nightmarish time for girls. Most of us don't escape unscathed. I remember the gauntlet from my adolescent years. It was a narrow path lined with boys lounging on their cars. We girls had to walk it to enter our high school. The boys would be leering, whistling, or making catcalls. What torture it was to walk past the boys, wondering if we would be teased for being fat, or flat-chested, or having a big behind. What self-consciousness and shame the experience produced in all of us.

By high school, the popular boys are those with status achieved through a combination of factors including athletic prowess, grades, looks, money, and personality. The popular girls are the most attractive ones. While women will continue to be evaluated in terms of appearance, looks will become even less important for men as their intelligence, drive, talent, and income-generating ability become paramount factors.

There is an old, extremely repulsive joke that demonstrates this point. "A doctor needed to hire a nurse. He interviewed three women, one who was skilled in surgery, one who was skilled in preventive medicine, and one who had an excellent bedside manner. Which one did he hire? The one with the good body."

The popular media—movies, television, advertising, and magazines—are the major promoters of lookism in women. Females are generally young, slim, handicap-free, and white. These are the women selected by powerful men as mates. Unattractive women are portrayed as unattractive people, as dull, obnoxious, or evil. Often, they are the butt of tasteless jokes, especially if they are fat.

Of course, many male stars are attractive. But some of our greatest male stars, such as James Cagney, Danny DeVito, Edward G. Robinson, and Dustin Hoffman, are decidedly not handsome. Character and talent count far more. Their intelligence, wit, and creativity give them power. Ordinary looking men with these qualities can become stars, even sex symbols.

A Nielsen poll reported that the average home has a television turned on eight hours a day. Sixty-nine percent of the female characters on television are thin; only 5 percent are overweight. Girls learn by watching television that being good-looking is often a sufficient condition for success. Slim women date movie stars and marry millionaires.

Most women and girls are not naturally as thin as our current ideal. Even those few who are don't take much pleasure in it. Jaimie Lee Curtis—whom *Esquire* once called "Hollywood's steamiest starlet"—dieted for eight months to be ready for her role in the movie *Perfect*. The same article quoted Curtis as saying she felt insecure about her looks. Demi Moore, who was recently photographed seminude for the cover of *Rolling Stone*, said in the accompanying interview, "I feel sexy getting dolled up. Being in panties and a cutout bra works for me. But I'm kind of a plain Jane. I don't have a good smile, I have no waist, and I'm never thin enough." Alicia Silverstone, the MTV icon who is now an actress, also felt badly about her body. In a magazine interview she revealed that "When I look in a mirror, sometimes it's very sad, because I feel like this fat, ugly blimp. And then I have to go out and be this beautiful girl."

Andrea Hadge, a New York psychotherapist who has worked with models, says that most are compulsive about diet and exercise. Many have bulimia and anorexia as well as other gastric disorders such as colitis and ulcers.

Too often looking "right" involves treating one's own body in punishing ways. Women go to sleep hungry, experience headaches from low blood sugar, and feel crabby and depressed from lack of nutrition. Still, most of us don't succeed at losing weight. Our hips remain too broad or our stomachs too round. Compared to our cultural goddesses, we are doomed to fall short of perfection.

The average person watches between 400 and 600 ads per day. Most of these ads show women who are pencil-thin, even anorexic. Sometimes the images are not even of real women. Instead, the photos in the ads are composites that combine the head of an adult woman, the torso of a young girl, and the legs of a boy. Women compare these images with their own bodies and feel anxious and inadequate. None of us has a body like these—they are not found in nature.

With each passing year the task of looking perfect becomes more difficult. Since 1950, our Miss Americas have grown slimmer while the average American woman has grown heavier. The average model is now 5 feet 10 inches tall and weighs 111 pounds. The average Playboy model weighs nearly 20 percent less than an average woman of the same height. As the disparity between real and ideal increases, the self-esteem of the average woman drops accordingly. The game is rigged and the odds against the players grow worse. But for most women it's the only game in town.

One survey of women of all ages revealed that only 4 percent felt comfortable about their weight. The other 96 percent felt overweight. One study found women more embarrassed to tell their weight than to answer questions such as "Are you homosexual?" or "How often do you masturbate?" Even elderly women remain haunted. In another study, older women were reported to fear weight gain more than any of the other physical changes associated with aging, except for memory loss.

To hate one's body is to hate oneself. Hating oneself makes

genuine acceptance of others impossible. Weight-obsessed women see other women as competition—or as overweight and disgusting—and they view men as harsh and judgmental. Their focus on weight also keeps them from attending to the development of their strengths and talents. When you overvalue the packaging, it's easy to undervalue the woman inside. Women are standing on the scales when they could be dancing, measuring their waistlines when they could be writing poetry.

Suggestions for Feeling Good About Your Body

1. When you look in a mirror, make sure to notice and remind yourself of what you like about your appearance. This may take some time and practice.

2. When you find yourself being critical of your appearance in the mirror, force yourself to turn away. Say firmly, "Body, you are mine. I like you."

3. Break the habit of comparing yourself to others in terms of appearance.

4. Don't criticize or comment on other women's appearances.

5. Learn to dress comfortably rather than "fashionably."

6. When you meet others, focus on something besides your appearance. Strive to be interesting, nurturing, witty, a good listener, and empathic.

7. Pay attention to the way media depictions of women influence your self-image, and stay away from media that makes you feel badly about your body and appearance.

8. Compliment girls and women for other things besides their physical appearance.

9. Learn to value yourself for other things besides your appearance. Keep track of your accomplishments and successes and remind yourself of them often.

10. Develop other interests besides your appearance. Focus on skills or activities that have nothing to do with your appearance.

Chapter Four

Why Diets Don't Work

"It goes hard with a woman who fails to adapt herself to
the prevalent masculine conception of her."
SOMERSET MAUGHAM

"People continually ruin their lives by persisting in
actions against which their senses rebel."
SOMERSET MAUGHAM

History of a Dieter

Loretta grew up in a small Kansas town. Her father sold automo-
biles and her mother was a homemaker. She was especially close
to her father and had memories of fishing, birdwatching, and play-
ing checkers with him. As a young girl, she sang in the church
youth choir and was a straight-A student.

Her father died when she was 12. Loretta remembers being
told of his death: "Mom sat down with us at breakfast and said
Dad had died in the night of a heart attack. Then she told us to get
dressed and go on to school. We didn't know any better, but everyone was surprised to see us there." She described a cold, hard feeling in her stomach the day she heard the news. That feeling didn't
go away until she left home six years later.

Loretta's mother found a job as a salesperson at Sears. She
had never been a strong person and her husband's death cata-
pulted her into lifelong malaise and hypochondria. She'd return

home from work each day and go straight to her bedroom. Many nights she wouldn't come back out.

Loretta and her brothers learned to care for themselves. Fortunately, they were all bright and enterprising. Dave developed a caustic wit and a poker face to hide his pain. Bob kept busy with sports and after-school jobs. Loretta kept up her studies, but withdrew from the family and community. She dropped out of choir. She spent her time outdoors bouncing a ball in the driveway and creating fantasy worlds in her mind. In one of them she was the beautiful daughter of a millionaire who liked to vacation in exotic resorts. In another, she was a movie star who made enough money to support her weary mother and send her brothers to college.

At age 18, Loretta graduated and moved to Lawrence to attend the University of Kansas. Her graduation picture shows a large, unsmiling girl staring straight into the camera. Her clothes are unfashionable and her hairstyle severe. Loretta described herself as quiet, studious, and afraid of men.

At the first dance in her dormitory she met Carl in a dark corner where they had both retired to hide. Standing together shyly, holding paper cups of warm punch, one of them managed to start a conversation. They had a lot in common. Both were from small towns, both were loners, and both were totally inexperienced with the opposite sex.

They dated and grew fond of one another. They were best friends, classmates, and then lovers. Their relationship protected them from the anxiety and risks of relationships with other students. They decided to study law and managed their schedules so they would be in the same classes. Like almost all students, they were poor, but they enjoyed those learning years.

The June after graduation, they married. Loretta and Carl moved to an Iowa town where Carl found work in a small investment company. Loretta decided to be lazy and spend the summer fixing up their place and learning her way around town. She planned to look for work in the fall. They were happy and excited to be in a new town and have some freedom from their families. They even had money.

It was in Iowa that Loretta began to diet. She'd always been heavy but it hadn't bothered her much. Now for some reason it did. Perhaps it was because Carl had a very slim secretary or maybe it was because she had a summer of free time to think. Her mother's words from her wedding day haunted her: "Don't gain any weight. Carl's a good-looking guy and he'll be able to find someone else if he wants." At the time she'd laughed it off as her neurotic mother talking, but now it hurt and angered her. She began to skip desserts.

Loretta went on her first diet in July. She bought a paperback with a slender model on the front and followed all the directions for a 1,000-calorie-a-day diet. Full of optimism, she'd sit down to a lunch of cottage cheese and tomato slices. At first she lost weight rapidly. Then her weight loss slowed down. She continued to eat her fresh spinach and broiled fish with lemon, but the diet no longer worked.

She felt miserable. Carl complained that she was tense and irritable and Loretta snapped that if he wanted her to be thin he would have to put up with it. He kept quiet. After two weeks she'd lost 10 pounds, most of it in the first three days. When she stopped dieting it came right back.

This was the first of what became a saga of diets. Loretta tried them all—the grapefruit diet, meatless diets, water pills, and wraparounds. She spent money for a special herbal diet consultant and joined a nutrition and weight loss clinic. Her conversation became a litany of information about diets and calories.

She also developed a cyclical pattern of eating. Weeks of deprivation would be followed by binges that left her devastated by self-loathing. She was either hungry and irritable or full and guilty. She was never happy.

Loretta had many angry feelings as she dieted. A rebellious little girl inside her kept saying, "Why can't you have what you want?" When she was hungry and nibbling on a carrot stick, she would find herself thinking, "Why are you torturing yourself? You deserve better." She became depressed. "I knew I would live longer if I lost weight, but I was so miserable that I didn't want to live longer." As for sex with Carl, she said, "Who feels sexy when they are starving to death?"

Loretta realized how much of her fun was food-related. She loved dinners in nice restaurants, get-togethers with friends for picnics and potlucks, and traveling. "Travel," she moaned, "is not fun without eating."

The boring sameness of the diets started to bother her. She

no longer enjoyed the foods she could eat. Most of all, Loretta missed cheese. She loved all kinds of cheese: brie, edam, stilton, and port wine cheddar. With her diets, she was reduced to eating an awful green and smelly cheese that had no cholesterol but tasted like soap.

Because she decided to lose weight before applying for jobs, Loretta didn't go to work in the fall. She did lose some weight, but as soon as she stopped dieting her weight would skyrocket. She watched as Carl polished off a quart of ice cream or a box of cookies and felt enraged. How could he eat what he wanted and not gain weight? If she even smelled dessert, she put on five pounds.

After months of dieting and bingeing, Loretta had changed. She was less energetic and outgoing. She was no longer so interested in law. Instead she planned her days around what she was and was not eating. She weighed herself every morning and felt anxious whatever the result. If she'd lost she was fearful she'd gain it back, and if she'd gained she was fearful she'd gain more. She also began seeing weight as the ultimate moral determinant—fat people were bad and thin people were good.

Her mother came to town and was appalled. Loretta had gained 30 pounds. Her mother accused her of having a cache of sweets stored somewhere. She suggested that if Loretta couldn't control herself she should have her jaws wired shut. That night Loretta cried herself to sleep.

After her mother returned home, Loretta made an appointment with me. She hoped a therapist could help her lose weight once and for all. During our first session she shared her history of failed diets. I asked her how the diets had affected the rest of her life.

As we talked over the next few months, Loretta discovered how out of control her eating had become. She realized how much her personality had changed since the diets began. She had grown moody and morbid, and life had become a grim business. Even her goals were different. "At one time I wanted to be a Supreme Court justice," Loretta lamented. "Now, I just want to wear a size 10 dress."

With encouragement, Loretta gained the courage to throw the scales away and trust her body to take care of itself. At first, Loretta was frightened. Dieting had become a way of life and she felt like someone jumping off of a cliff. She was terrified she would inflate into a Hindenberg-sized blimp.

For a while she did gain, but after a few months her weight stabilized. It was higher than she wanted, but at least she was no longer food-obsessed. Loretta also began an exercise program that helped with her depression.

For the first time in her life, Loretta examined her feelings. Instead of burying them deep inside, she talked. She wept for the loss of her father and raged at her mother for abandoning her when she most needed her. She admitted she was deeply fearful of other people and had avoided meeting strangers. When she received her law degree, she had not been confident enough to move into the world of professional adults. Rather than tackle that, she focused on her weight. Weight had become the absolute and only measure of her worth.

Loretta decided that she would no longer use her weight as an excuse to avoid doing things and that she would start to develop herself as a person. She bought a professional suit and started sending out resumés. She joined a women's choir and sang for the first time since her father's death. Once again, she and Carl were going out on dates and laughing and joking around at home. Her interest in sex returned.

Fortunately, Loretta helped herself out of the diet trap. She remained a heavy woman, but she no longer let her weight determine her worth. She had lost two years of her life to diets, which is actually much less time than most women lose. Once again, she was on a healthy path. She saw herself as a person, not as a body. Life was to be lived and savored.

The "Set Point" Limit

At any given time, 50 percent of all American women report they are on a diet. Most of them are doomed to fail. Only 5 percent of all dieters can successfully keep off as much as 20 pounds. Yet, in spite of the scientific evidence, we persist in the belief that individuals are responsible for their own body size. It's a convenient assumption for the thin, but for the heavy, its effects are devastating.

To diet is to limit eating in order to lose weight. Diets are based on the assumption that if your food intake equals your energy expenditure, your weight will remain constant. It follows that to lose weight a person needs either to increase her energy expenditure (exercise) or decrease her consumption (diet).

This formula has proven to be too simple and linear to be useful. It has been replaced by what is popularly known as the "set point" theory. This theory postulates that there is an internal control system that dictates how much body fat a given individual should carry. This amount of fat varies greatly from person to person, but stays remarkably constant for any given individual over time.

There is some evidence that diets can raise an individual's set point and exercise may lower it slightly. However, the set point is mostly determined by genetic factors and is relatively impervious to conscious control. Researchers now believe that 70 percent of the influences on an adult's weight are hereditary. One client commented that after years of bingeing and purging she weighed exactly what she did when she started.

The set point determines the body's physical reactions to food. If food consumption increases, metabolism speeds up; if food consumption decreases, metabolism slows down. All things considered, the set point is a useful adaptive mechanism for a creature with an erratic food supply.

Think of an aborigine woman going long days without food until there is a kill. After the kill she is likely to eat until she's satiated. Without some sort of metabolic regulation, she would likely starve during the time between kills. For days after a feast, even when food was available, she would be too full to eat. This built-in variation in our metabolic rate enables humans to make the most efficient use of their food supply, which has been a scarce resource through much of our history.

The set point even appears to influence the conscious mind. When the level of body fat falls below a certain point, the mind becomes utterly preoccupied with food. In 1944, research was conducted on conscientious objectors at the University of Minnesota. The study was designed to learn how starvation affected the mind and behavior of human beings. Volunteers in the study ate normal 3500-calorie-a-day meals for three months, while their moods and behaviors were carefully monitored. Then, for roughly six months, their diet was restricted to 1800 calories a day. Both psychological and physical changes were carefully noted.

At first, the men lost weight rapidly. After two months they had lost about half their body fat. Their behavior changed radically as this occurred. Cheerful, active men slowed down and became apathetic and lethargic. They withdrew from all social occasions except mealtimes. The men experienced constant ravenous hunger that would not allow them to concentrate or relax. Amazingly, this hunger stayed with the men even after they resumed a 5000-calorie-a-day diet.

Researchers concluded that these men remained food-obsessed until they returned to their prediet weights and original amount of fat tissue. The number of calories eaten per day was largely irrelevant to the feelings of hunger. Rather, the missing fat determined their psychological states.

A study by E. A. H. Sims at the Vermont State Prison documented the same effect from an opposite point of view. Volunteers tried to gain weight by overeating. For over six months the men ate twice as much as they usually did. In spite of eating seven meals a day, it was very difficult for them to gain weight. The men had to overeat by an average of 2000 calories a day to keep gaining weight. One man could only gain weight by eating over 7000 calories a day!

The men found overeating extremely unpleasant. Food lost its appeal and even thoughts of food made the men nauseous. It was as if their bodies were screaming, "Don't eat." Every participant asked at one time or another to be excused from the project. The side effects of overeating—sluggishness, pessimism, and irritability—were tough to handle.

The set point mechanism does not discriminate between dieting and unplanned starvation. People on diets will experience the same obsessions as starvation victims. They will become lethargic, depressed, and irritable. Losing weight becomes virtually impossible as metabolism slows down. The further dieters move from the set point, the more difficult losing weight becomes. When they stop the diet, the weight leaps back on.

As a group, fat people do not eat more than thin people. In fact, scientific studies suggest just the opposite is true. Susan Wooley reported that in 19 of 20 studies obese people as a group ate less than thin people. A. J. Stunkard and his associates recorded the caloric intake of people eating in fast-food restaurants. They found that obese customers (those judged to be 30 percent over the ideal body weight) had eaten no more than the thinnest customers. A similar study recorded the eating of obese and nonobese adolescent girls at camp. Much to the researcher's surprise, the obese girls, as a group, ate less than the slim and normal-weight girls. Certainly, some obese people have hearty appetites. But so do average-weight and thin people.

What is more likely is that many large people have set points that keep their weight higher than average. Any attempts they make to lose weight by dieting are likely to fail. Exercise may lower their set points slightly, but generally most heavy people can expect to stay heavy.

What can change is our cultural attitudes toward heavy people. We can be less punitive and condemning. If being heavy is not seen as a social disgrace or a character flaw, then heavy women can begin to feel proud of their large, good bodies. They won't need to try to change the unchangeable. Women like Loretta can be healthy and accept themselves as they are.

Suggestions for Avoiding the Binge-Starve Cycle

1. Don't go on a diet.

2. Know the basic facts about nutrition. Read the labels before you buy groceries and make conscious choices about your purchases. Eat three meals daily and healthy snacks whenever you are hungry.

3. Write down a history of your attempts to lose weight, and make a list of the "side effects" your efforts have had on your life.

4. Make another list of the positive changes you would make in your life if you felt more confident and happy. Think about how your concerns with your weight make it more difficult to achieve your goals.

5. Don't listen to others talk about diets and weight. Anxiety is infectious.

6. Move whenever you can. This not only includes daily exercise, but also choosing to walk rather than ride at every opportunity. Seek to exercise rather than seeking to avoid eating. For example, take the stairs instead of the elevator, park

farther away from the entrance you use and walk, and go for a stroll after dinner rather than sitting in the living room.

7. Don't buy clothes that are too small and hope to shrink into them. This is setting yourself up for failure and disappointment.

8. Don't be lookist about others. Do your part to break our national obsession with physical appearance. Don't make lookist comments or judgments about others.

9. Don't let your insecurity about your appearance be an excuse to keep you from doing what you want. For example, go swimming today, not when you lose 10 pounds. Try out for a play. Don't wait for that mythical time in the future when you will be thin or put off activities until you lose weight. It's important to become a useful, productive person now.

CHAPTER FIVE

Solutions that Don't Work

Every year women spend billions of dollars on diet books, low-calorie foods, weight-loss drugs, clinics, and surgeries. Every month a new diet is "discovered"—ranging from the Beverly Hills diet to the Scarsdale, Herbal Life, or Single Woman's diets. Dieting potions as phony as snake oil abound. There are prescription medicines and appetite suppressants that are addictive and dangerous. There is the fat-burning grapefruit pill, or the Japanese super-pill, "so effective, so relentless in its awesome attack on bulging fatty deposits that it has virtually eliminated the need to diet."

Women's magazines are filled with weight loss aids. They feature 11 times more articles on dieting than do magazines for a general audience. Recently, I glanced through one and found all kinds of medications for sale. There were fiber pills from Europe that "give you a pleasant feeling of fullness before meals." Another medication advertisement purported to let you eat all you want and still lose weight. "Lose weight whether you exercise or not," shouted the ad. It claimed this pill suppressed calorie absorption and warned that you might become too thin if you used it for long. There were assorted caffeine tablets to suppress the appetite, and a pill that supposedly would control hunger and speed up metabolism. Does that sound safe?

In this same magazine, another ad promised a weight loss of 16 pounds a week. The ad for the amazing fat-attacker pill claimed, "Do it right now and let this be the first day of an exciting new life for you."

There was a program for fanny improvement that promised you a tighter, rounder, firmer bottom in 30 days. There were "take-it-off-and-keep-it-off" camps that promised you would have fun and lose 25 to 45 pounds in a week. And there were cassette tapes, supposedly made by psychologists, that helped you "sublimate" your hunger. All of this was expensive, by the way.

Women are desperate and will try almost anything to lose weight. Unfortunately, most diets fail. A 1994 survey reported that 90 percent of dieters regain all the weight they lost within five years. When these diets fail, we blame ourselves, not the diet.

Many women rely on diet books for advice. What does the literature of weight loss teach us about our bodies? The recurring themes lead to myths about dieting, women, and their bodies:

Myth #1. Fat is ugly, disgusting, and a cause for self-loathing. Being fat is described as a horrible fate. As one author of a popular diet book writes, "I lie in terror that I won't see my hip bones when I look in the mirror." Being fat is seen as a sufficient cause for shame and guilt. One doctor prescribed a rigid 1200-calorie-a-day regimen with each nibble spelled out because "so many overweight people have no self-control." This same doctor gave out charts of perfect measurements for women of all heights. His measurements even included ankle and wrist size. Presumably, he selected a set of measurements that were pleasing to him and assumed they must be "perfect." This doctor's message was clear—that by exerting enough self-control to follow his diet, women could become perfect. By implication, those who didn't lose weight were self-indulgent slugs.

Myth #2. If you are not slender, you should be angry at yourself. One book suggested standing naked in front of a mirror and telling yourself off for overeating. It recommended calling oneself "Fatso" or other epithets, and focusing on particular mounds of fat as evidence of one's failure. Unfortunately, most women don't need to be taught how to run themselves down. This skill is already well-developed.

Myth #3. You will be a social outcast unless you lose weight. The discriminatory status quo that judges women according to their physical appearance is accepted without question. One author wrote, "Picture yourself doing well on a job that you wouldn't dare aspire to because of your weight." By not challenging the unfairness of a job market that penalizes women with certain body types, these books give tacit consent to such practices.

Myth #4. Appearance is a woman's most important personal attribute; total preoccupation with weight is reasonable. Weight loss is seen as a valuable enough goal to justify marked food deprivation and physical and psychological discomfort. One doctor encourages women to start their diets by eating no solid food for three days. He encourages women to ignore the side effects of fasting such as dizziness, tiredness, and diarrhea. He states, rather too optimistically, that no one has ever been hurt by a diet. Worthwhile goals like feeling useful, confident, or satisfied are subordinated to being slender.

Myth #5. Do not trust yourself to make decisions about your eating. One author suggests, "Give up the instant gratification of food for the long-term gratification of a new body and a new life." Women are encouraged to mislabel their internal cues. One author writes, "re-define hunger as good, not bad. Your body is burning up fat." Another author writes, "Your growling stomach is nature's way of applauding your work." In each of these examples, women are trained to devalue their knowledge of their own bodies and their ability to make good decisions for themselves.

Myth #6. Fasting and bingeing is an acceptable way to diet. One author suggests losing 10 pounds and then bingeing to reward oneself. Another recommends eating all you want for 10 days and then fasting for 5. She jokingly calls this the rhythm method of "girth control." The message is that any means, no matter how extreme or unhealthy, is worth trying in an effort to lose weight.

One book even encouraged purging. The author suggests the use of laxatives the first few days of a diet. She minimizes the side effects, and says not to be alarmed if your weight fluctuates rapidly from day to day. She continues, "Don't worry if you have loose bowel movements from time to time. The more time spent on the pot the better."

Many so-called diet experts are out of touch with recent medical research. Their advice is useless at best; at worst it is harmful or even deadly. Yet their books sell. The sad irony is that good books are available that offer sensible advice about exercise and nutrition, but they continue to be overlooked by women searching for solutions to their weight problems.

With such extreme and unhealthy attitudes being fostered among women, it's not surprising that many are willing to consider more radical medical and surgical solutions. One such invention is a stomach balloon that is inserted through the mouth in a deflated state. Once in the stomach, it is blown up and positioned. This balloon gives people a feeling of fullness and works as an appetite suppressant. It was cleared by the Food and Drug Administration (FDA) in the fall of 1985 and is considered by some doctors safer than other surgical methods. Unfortunately, many complications have been documented. Stomach ulcers and gastrointestinal blockage, which is potentially fatal, may develop.

Another unfortunate trend is the increase in cosmetic surgeries. A wide variety of fat-removing surgeries are now available, including body contours, tummy tucks, collagen removal, and lipectomies. Most of the women who seek these surgeries have no gross physical deformities. Rather they have bodies that are beginning to show the natural effects of aging. Or, they are younger and want to look absolutely perfect.

I have noticed among my clients a tendency to consider these surgeries following a divorce. Women often focus on their fat or sagginess when they feel emotionally vulnerable. Especially when they think of dating, they are overwhelmed by anxiety about their appearance. They know it will be important on the dating scene and they try to ready themselves for the competition.

By far the most common cosmetic surgery is the suction lipectomy. Thousands of these procedures are performed in this country every year, mostly in California, Florida, Texas, and New York. This procedure actually suctions the fat cells out of such areas as the stomach, buttocks, and thighs. It's an expensive and painful surgery. Women are bruised for six weeks, and numb in the area affected for up to six months. The complications can include nerve damage, infections, vessel damage, and skin that ripples permanently.

The most radical of all cosmetic surgeries are those that alter the gastrointestinal tract so that food is not absorbed by the stomach. The two most common forms are the gastric bypass, which shunts most food directly to the colon before absorption occurs, and stomach stapling, which renders most of the stomach useless and reduces its holding capacity to a few ounces. Both of these surgeries have significant mortality rates. They are painful, debilitating, and often create lifelong health problems for women. Serious side effects occur in 60 percent of all cases. Furthermore, in many cases the surgery is not effective. After an initial weight loss while hospitalized and convalescing, many women regain the pounds they had lost. In addition, many women develop bizarre eating practices to cope with their unnatural and inefficient digestive system. Twenty-five percent of all women eventually must have the surgery reversed. Even the "successful" surgeries can convert a healthy obese person into an unhealthy thin one.

The last few chapters have explored the messages women get about the importance of being thin, and the radical solutions they try to avoid having round bodies. Most of us have seen diets damage the health, temperament, and self-esteem of ourselves or friends. Yet, because of our fears, many of us continue to try these faulty solutions. To become thin, some women will even risk and lose their lives. This useless destruction will continue as long as the cost of being overweight is social suicide.

CHAPTER SIX

Clients with Bulimia

Cassandra

When I met Cassandra she was a slender blonde student who had just turned 20. Dressed in punk-style clothes and an enormous floppy hat, she sat defiantly in my office. Her first comment was that she thought shrinks were stupid and she had only come because her father had made her come. Reluctantly she explained that he'd found her vomiting after last Sunday's meal. He was concerned that she had an eating disorder. She thought she had a slight problem with food, but she could take care of it whenever she wanted. I suggested we talk of other things and decide later about her eating.

Somewhat begrudgingly, Cassandra told me about herself. She was the youngest of six children in a Catholic family. Her father was a physician and her mother was a nurse who had turned homemaker after the children came. She described a "Father Knows Best" kind of childhood. She was the pet in a family where her mother often had fresh-baked cookies waiting after school. She'd always been popular and a good student. Until junior high school, her most traumatic childhood memory was having chicken pox.

Like many girls, Cassandra had trouble in junior high. Her body developed slowly and she was nicknamed "the board" because of her flat chest. She felt lost and insecure in ninth grade until she met a popular boy. Doug was an athlete who had a special way of teasing her that made her feel loved and safe. Once she and Doug started dating, her rocky transition into adolescence smoothed out. Cassandra became an award-winning artist and a cheerleader. Her coolness quotient soared. With Doug by her side, she was confident and joyous.

When Cassandra was sixteen she discovered that Doug was sleeping with another girl. She broke off the relationship at once, but she couldn't stop thinking about him. They had been so close and had never argued. Agonizing over the question of why Doug had strayed, Cassandra decided that if she had been thinner, he wouldn't have left. Doug had often teased her about her "big behind."

For the first time in her life, Cassandra dieted. In the beginning she just skipped dessert, but later she restricted herself to 1000-calorie-a-day diets. Sometimes Cassandra couldn't stand the "rabbit food" and binged on ice cream or fried chicken. Once, after a particularly large binge, she felt anxious about her weight. She knew a girl at school who vomited to lose weight and Cassandra decided to give it a try. It was difficult and disgusting to make herself vomit, but Cassandra liked the fact that she didn't gain weight. Two weeks later she repeated the pattern.

By the time she was seventeen, she was unable to make it through a day without bingeing and purging. Gradually her social life changed to accommodate her eating habits. She no longer ate with others unless she could vomit in private afterwards. Often she turned down dates so she would have more time to binge. Her energy level dropped, as did her grades.

When Cassandra graduated from high school, she went to college and moved into an apartment near campus. She decided to major in French because it was easy. Watercolors of butterflies that she had painted in high school decorated the walls of her place. She no longer painted as she had neither the time nor energy. Her money was spent for food instead of art supplies. She had become a loner and rarely attended a movie or concert. Her one pleasure was eating.

Cassandra binged two or three times a day and usually consumed 5000 to 10,000 calories per binge. Like most bulimics, Cassandra was obsessed with food and terrified of weight gain. She did manage to attend most of her classes and study enough to make passing grades, but much of her time was spent buying, cooking, or eating food. Then she purged, usually by gagging herself and vomiting, but sometimes by taking laxatives. Afterwards, she had the typical bulimic's "hangover" with all of its symptoms, including a stomachache and bloodshot eyes. She became chronically weak and lethargic.

What follows are two fairly typical pages from Cassandra's food journal:

Thursday, June 4

8:30	Half a grapefruit with tea and artificial sweetener
1:35	Ham sandwich, apple, 12-ounce bag of Doritos, quart of strawberry ice cream, can of Pringles, bottle of Spanish olives, 8-ounce container of cottage cheese with a can of peaches, cookies
3:30	Vomit
8:00	Lettuce wedge with low-cal dressing, piece of chicken, two-pound box of saltines, popcorn, three Mars bars, nachos, cookies, loaf of raisin bread
9:30	Vomit

Friday, June 5

9:15	Tea with artificial sweetener and one half apple
11:30	Small bag of popcorn, no butter, orange, tuna fish sandwich, ice cream bar, cocoa, bag of malted milk balls, box of granola bars
1:00	Vomit
5:30	Lite beer, carrot sticks
6:30	Bowl of chili, salad with low-cal dressing
7:30	Can of ravioli, can of chili, two boxes of animal crackers, loaf of banana bread, bag of corn puffs
9:00	Vomit

Her pattern was to either nibble or binge. Even the small meals that Cassandra attempted made her anxious. She was so frightened of weight gain that she couldn't relax or study. Usually she began with small servings of healthy foods and then spiraled out of control on junk foods.

This bingeing and purging had stolen hours out of Cassandra's life. At the time she wrote these entries, Cassandra was still chained to her eating disorder. Here's what she wrote one night after waking and bingeing:

How did I get so weird? My life revolves around eating and ridding myself of food. My days are a waste. I waste time, money, and energy—and I'm wasting myself.

I can't believe I've managed to stay in school all these years. There hasn't been a day when I haven't been tormented by the frustration I create for myself about where, when, and what I shall eat.

I have potential that if released could do amazing things. But it's trapped inside me. I am a suffering, driven, and depressed person. I remember myself as an involved, bright, laughing girl who made the people around me laugh. I used to be proud of my talents and willing to work on them.

But somehow I began to change. That sparkly person disappeared. Who I was became how I looked. Finally, all that mattered was my weight.

Freedom for me is having no concern for how I look or what I eat. Probably the stupidest, most shallow definition of freedom ever written.

Fortunately, once she faced her problem Cassandra was a hard worker. She kept her journal religiously and followed all the homework assignments that were designed to help her stop bingeing and purging. Slowly she learned to tolerate the anxiety of having a small normal meal. She stopped weighing herself daily and gradually reduced the number of binges and purges per week. She walked and swam and developed new ways of coping with stress.

She educated herself on bulimia and even started a small support group of women from her campus. After 15 months of hard work, she is symptom-free and once again dating and doing her lovely watercolors. Most important, she is no longer a prisoner of her addiction. She can eat when she is hungry and stop before she loses control. Once again she enjoys life with all its depth and complexity.

Carla

Carla was the youngest child in an unusual family. Her father was a wealthy alcoholic and her mother was a beautiful but miserable socialite. The children in the family were talented, but confused and rebellious. They had a pattern of failing in school and running away from their chaotic family. When Carla's last brother, David, left home at 18 to join the army, she was alone with her parents.

With no brothers and sisters to act as buffers, Carla felt trapped with two adults who hated each other. She would lie in bed at night and hear her parents shouting. Her father was often drunk and her mother scared and bitter. Sometimes her father would hit her mother.

She loved both her parents, but she couldn't depend on them. Other kids her age didn't seem to have problems like hers. She turned to David's drug-using buddies for support and sympathy. David's girlfriend, Terri, became her "big sister." She listened to her problems, gave her advice on clothes, and bought her candy and pop. Terri also taught Carla to smoke dope.

That summer Carla turned 13. She ate a lot of candy. Dope made her hungry. She started her periods that fall and gained weight around the hips. Terri suggested they go on a diet together.

The first time they fasted for two days, and Carla lost six pounds. She fainted in the restroom at school, but no one knew the reason. Fasting continued to be Carla's favorite way of dieting. It had to be all or none. If she ate candy she wanted a bag. Better to skip food totally than risk losing control. Her parents knew she was skipping meals, but they weren't alarmed. She looked fine and besides, her mother dieted all the time too.

When a fast ended, Terri and Carla would celebrate with an ice cream cone or a pizza. One Saturday night, they were at Terri's watching TV. They started on chocolate chip cookies, then moved on to ice cream, sugar-coated cereals, chocolates, and granola bars. They giggled and stuffed themselves, and at the same time, were surprised that they were doing this. When it was over they felt awful. Carla's stomach hurt and she felt like vomiting. Terri said, "Hey, good idea. Then we won't gain weight." They thought they'd made a wonderful discovery. Magic. A way to pig out and still be thin.

When I met Carla, she had been through an inpatient program for bulimia. Her parents had noticed her problem when 50 dollars worth of groceries disappeared in one night and, at the advice of their physician, they hospitalized Carla. She made some progress in the hospital, but rapidly returned to her bingeing when released. When we first discussed her eating, Carla was bingeing up to five times a day, eating as much as 30,000 calories. She was also hooked on pot, alcohol, and diet pills.

In spite of these horrendous problems, Carla was a likable person. She was smart, sensitive, and creative. She was lovely too, with alabaster skin and long black hair. Unless you looked closely, you wouldn't notice her bloodshot eyes or the puffiness under her skin.

We talked about Carla's current situation. She was no longer attending public schools, because she'd been expelled for drugs. She no longer could fall asleep without food or drugs. Her digestive system was sluggish. Worst of all, she no longer had fun. As Carla put it, "I'm just going through the motions."

Carla began a food journal. Except for binges, she never ate. Her diet was exclusively fast foods and junk foods. My first recommendation was that she bring a healthy lunch to our sessions and we would eat together. That was tough for Carla but she did it. After a few months she could eat small lunches and snacks without bingeing. Gradually, she cut down on the number of binges. She started jogging.

We talked about other issues. Carla looked at how her father's drinking had affected her family. She started attending Al-Anon and eventually her mother accompanied her to a meeting. We talked about the pain of a destructive family. When things seemed out of control, Carla had tried desperately to control the one thing she could, her weight.

Carla still has a long way to go. She worries about her appearance and turns to food when she is stressed. But I think she'll make it. She's off drugs now and reports that controlling drugs and alcohol is easy compared to stopping bingeing. She very much wants to be free of her addiction. Her goal for herself is to be "normal." Someday I think she'll be extraordinary.

Roberta

Roberta came to my office in faded jeans and tennis shoes. She chain-smoked and had the hoarse, sexy laugh of a barroom singer. Without a hint of self-pity, she explained that she was working in a factory and supporting five children on her wages. Her husband had left her five years ago and since then she'd handled most family responsibilities alone. She was proud of her children, the "rug rats" as she called them, who were doing well in school and popular with their classmates. Though lacking in formal education, Roberta was well-read. She loved the classics and wished more women at the factory read good books.

She was isolated. Few men wanted to date a smart woman with five children and she had little time or energy for female friends. After the children's needs were met there was no money left to spend on her entertainment. Every night Roberta came home from the factory and walked into a messy house with five noisy kids. She fixed supper for them, helped with their homework, picked up the house, did laundry, and made lunches for the next day. Then at ten o'clock, with the children finally in bed, she binged.

Roberta told me, "It's the only thing besides reading that I do for myself. I feel ashamed of this habit. I'm too smart to act this stupid, but I need something. It's the only time I feel okay." Afterwards she vomited so she wouldn't gain weight.

Roberta came into therapy because she could no longer afford the binges. She felt guilty for eating food the children wanted or needed. "I'll go through half a week's groceries in a night. Then we eat macaroni and cheese." Fortunately, her factory had a benefits package that reimbursed her for a private therapist.

She knew she binged to reward herself, so we worked on developing ways Roberta could be good to herself. Before she could do this, Roberta needed help with the children. I encouraged her to ask her ex-husband for more support and also to rely on her parents who agreed to watch the kids one night a week.

At first, she was reluctant, but soon she was enjoying the extra time with books, walks in the park, and movies. Roberta joined a support group where the women encouraged her to make the children help out more at home. Most important, the women in the group cared about her and offered to listen when she needed an adult's ear.

We agreed that for Roberta bingeing meant nurturance. She was always the responsible person. There was no one to take care of her. Food had become her way of comforting herself.

One small assignment helped her stop bingeing forever. I told her whenever she felt like bingeing, she should call me or a friend from the support group. She should tell that person she needed some TLC ("Tender Loving Care") and then talk. For Roberta, being listened to and valued became even more rewarding than food. Roberta began to make friends and was eventually free of her addiction.

Connie

Connie was a small, silent woman married to a protective and autocratic husband. They were fundamentalist Christians who believed that the husband should be the leader and decision-maker in the family. Connie was reared to believe and still believes that men are to be obeyed and that good women don't feel or express anger.

Connie and her husband came in weekly. Connie listened respectfully while Bill told me how well things were going. He thought she was wonderful and swore that they never disagreed. He said earnestly, "Connie is so easy to get along with."

They had come to me for help with bulimia. Connie binged and purged as many as four times a day. She waited until Bill left for work and then slipped down to the bakery for two dozen sugar donuts and several loaves of bread. She told the saleslady it was for a church meeting.

At night she encouraged Bill to go to the movies or to visit his relatives, anything to get him out of the house so she could make pancakes or buy junk food and binge. Bill could hardly believe she was bulimic since he'd never seen her binge or vomit. But he did know they had no savings and that Connie had been hospitalized twice with bulimia-related medical problems.

I suggested that her self-destructive eating was related to her low self-esteem and feelings of powerlessness and rage. She denied it demurely and asked, "How can that be when Bill and I are so happy?"

At first, work with Connie was difficult and not very successful. Even with me, she was secretive about her eating. She tried to complete her assignments, but never was quite able to make it. I would ask her to bring in an eating journal and she'd forget. I would encourage her to express her feelings to Bill and she'd go a month without having a feeling.

Connie probably would have stopped therapy in frustration

except that she wanted a baby. She and Bill knew that she had to recover before they could consider a pregnancy. So we plugged away. Finally, Connie told Bill that she was miffed about something he had done. He was confused and angry and Connie backed down immediately. But Bill came through, suggesting there were worse things than conflict, like bulimia.

In the office we began to work on conflict resolution skills. Every week Connie and Bill would bring in a conflict to discuss. At first, these were small conflicts, such as who read the paper first, but later they expanded to cover their main areas of disagreement. Connie became more assertive. She asked Bill for more money and for a vote in planning their outings. When she did this, she turned tomato red and breathed in a funny, irregular way, but she did it. Bill was angry at first. Then he surprised us both by saying he found Connie more interesting since she had started being honest.

After six months, Connie applied for a job in a health food store. She was hired and earned her own money. Bill didn't like the idea of his wife working, but he liked the extra money and the fact that it kept Connie from bingeing during the day. She loved being out and meeting new people. She especially liked helping women with their nutritional planning. Slowly, she began to help herself. Her own bingeing decreased as her self-esteem and self-protective skills increased.

There are many similar stories. Joyce, for example, was a charming professional woman who made a good salary and was often on television. No doubt, her appearance helped her get to the top of her field. Beautifully groomed and wearing three-hundred-dollar suits, Joyce came in weekly for help with her bulimia. Her interests had dwindled to only two areas: her weight and eating. She had stopped having sexual fantasies two years earlier, and now fantasized only about food. She avoided certain streets because there were bakeries or fast food restaurants on them. She equated her professional success with her thinness and she was sure that even gaining a few pounds would jeopardize her job. I couldn't reassure her that it wasn't so.

Then there's Sandy, an energetic, red-headed school teacher who felt especially guilty about her bulimia because she was a lesbian feminist. She felt feminists should be immune to this disease. After all, she wasn't concerned about men's opinions of her attractiveness. But she was addicted to the binge-purge cycle. After school every day she rushed home to gorge on chocolate and peanut butter. She avoided a long-term relationship because she feared her bulimia would be discovered.

All kinds of women from all kinds of backgrounds are bulimics. Like divorce, the problem is widespread, but the pain is individual and often unshared. Each woman feels responsible for her condition even though to a large extent, cultural conditions have created this nightmarish problem. In the next chapter, we'll look at the reasons why culturally-induced bulimia has become such a widespread illness.

CHAPTER SEVEN

Bulimia—The Food Addiction

Bulimia is an epidemic of the 1980s and 1990s. Twenty years ago many mental health professionals had not heard of the problem. Now we seem to encounter bulimic women everywhere. College sororities and dormitories are overwhelmed with victims. By now, 8 to 20 percent of all high school girls are bulimic. Junior high school girls are throwing up in groups in the restrooms after lunch. I have a bulimic friend, a bulimic neighbor, and a caseload increasingly filled with bulimic clients. Psychologists are now estimating the incidence rate for bulimia among college-aged women to be as high as one in every four or five. Women face a new and terrible problem in our society, and unless we take steps to contain it, the illness will continue to spread.

According to the *Diagnostic and Statistical Manual for Psychologists*, a woman must demonstrate the following symptoms to be diagnosed as bulimic:

1. Recurrent binge eating

2. Eating that is abnormal and feels out of control

3. Depression and self-deprecating thoughts following a binge

4. Any three of the following five characteristics:

    a. Consumption of high calorie junk food during a binge

    b. Hiding food and secretive eating

    c. Termination of the binge by abdominal pain, sleep, or vomiting

   d.   Repeated weight loss and attempts to control weight by cathartics and diuretics

   e.   Weight fluctuations of over 10 pounds in one year

Women who do not meet all of the above criteria may still have a bulimic pattern of eating.

Although this chapter will discuss bulimia in women, some men, such as dancers and wrestlers, are also at risk. This makes perfect sense: for these men, weight control is necessary to attain their goals. Like women, they are often encouraged to undertake frequent and radical diets. In some cases, men substitute food for alcohol when they give up drinking. I knew of a salesman who drank in hotel rooms far from home. He had joined Alcoholics Anonymous (AA) and quit drinking, but he binged on room service meals so that he could sleep.

The Origins of Bulimia

How does this psychologically damaging, physically dangerous, and expensive problem develop? Among my clients, a common trigger for the development of bulimia is rejection by a man. This rejection prompts a search for the cause of the rejection. Often, the woman can find no cause in her behavior. She's been sexually available, accommodating, and uncomplaining. So she decides it must have been her weight. Mr. Right wouldn't have walked away if she'd been 10 pounds lighter or had a flatter stomach.

But there are other causes as well. In general, women experience some kind of failure and attribute that failure to their weight. They think that if they can control their weight, they will be able to get what they want. Partly, this thought may stem from a lack of self-confidence. Partly, it is a realistic perception. Women who are thin are more likely to get what they want from our culture.

Naturally, this attribution makes the woman want to lose weight. So she'll begin to diet compulsively. At first, she'll starve herself, keeping an iron grip on her impulse to eat. Unfortunately, her self-control is bound to fail eventually. She's hungry *and* miserable, and when she fails it's likely to be in a big way. Like all ravenous people, she will gorge herself. Feeling guilty about the calories she has consumed, and anxious about the possibility of gaining weight, she will try purging.

Any diet can be a first step in the direction of an eating disorder. Once a woman has lost touch with her own internal hunger mechanism, she is vulnerable to other influences on her eating behavior. Some diets even encourage bulimic eating patterns. Alternating food deprivation with food orgies, the dieter will gain and lose the same 15 pounds over and over. Slowly the diet–no diet process accelerates until the woman is alternating binge and fast days. The dieter is now only a step away from bulimia. For some women, it is just a question of time before the binge–purge cycle overwhelms their normal eating patterns.

Often the suggestion of a friend, such as Carla's friend Terri, plays a role in the development of bulimia. Weight-obsessed women offer "help" to other weight-obsessed women. "Throw up and you won't gain weight." This word-of-mouth transmission of bulimia occurs frequently in college dorms and sororities.

College girls tend to be hypercritical of their bodies, stressed by academic and social pressures, and eager for male approval. Most are body-conscious calorie counters. Binge-and-starve eating habits are common. Young women who live in dormitories often complain that the bathrooms smell like vomit. In some sororities, the girls study together, binge together, and then go as a group to the restrooms to vomit. Some try a few times, get scared, and stop—while others go on to full-fledged bulimia.

Many bulimics are women with traditional values who have accepted society's definition of their role hook, line, and scales. They may overtly condemn people who judge others by appearance, but they are determined to please them. They very much want a relationship with a man. Once involved, they tend to be passive-dependent and allow the man to be in charge. Partly, this comes from their eagerness for male approval. Partly, it's because the bulimic woman herself doesn't know what she wants. She has focused so exclusively on her appearance that she is unsure of her own inner nature.

It is impossible to overestimate the bulimic woman's terror of gaining weight. Over time this disease causes a distorted body image. Women come to see themselves as gross and disgusting. They are convinced that only their bulimia keeps them from obesity.

In this sense bulimic women often don't want to lose their problem. They see a worse danger looming ahead—themselves as three-hundred-pound social pariahs. They know how ravenous and out of control they are when eating. No matter how disabling the bulimia has become, obesity seems like a worse fate.

Ironically, this obsession with weight gain or loss has little effect on actual weight. Carla's and Roberta's weights remained the same year after year no matter what they did to their bodies. Cassandra once said to me, "It's crazy. After seven years of doing nothing but worry about my weight, I weigh just what I did when I started."

How Bulimia Affects Women

Sadly, the relationships these women are trying to achieve give them little pleasure. They are too weight- and body-obsessed to actually enjoy another person. Even sex is not good for most bulimics. First of all, they are too aware of their body's defects to relax. As Lisa put it, "I'm always thinking about my fat instead of how I feel. I'm worried about what my partner is thinking, too." Second, most bulimics suffer from *anhedonia*, the inability to experience pleasure. All of a bulimic woman's emotional and physical energy is focused on weight and eating. Eating is no longer pleasurable. Instead, it's compulsive, animalistic and guilt-inducing. Nothing is fun.

Third, bulimic women are physically ill. Tired and drained from bingeing and purging, they have no energy for sex or any other physical activity. Most bulimic women stop having sexual fantasies. The prize that they may have won with their thinness—a man that wants them for a sex partner—has become a hollow victory. I'm reminded of a line by T. S. Eliot: "Lips that would kiss make prayers to broken stones."

Many serious health problems are associated with bulimia. Dehydration and the consequent electrolytic imbalance can require hospitalization and the use of intravenous fluids. Chronic gagging leads to throat and esophagus injuries. Repeated gorging and vomiting or the chronic overuse of laxatives cause stomach, bowel, and gastrointestinal tract disorders. Dental problems, such as the decalcification of the teeth, are frequent. Emetics, which are medications used to induce vomiting, are especially dangerous.

Ipecac, the most common emetic, is a poison that has led to death by congestive heart failure in some women.

Bulimia poses serious health problems for pregnant women and their babies. Unfortunately, the age group at risk for bulimia is also the age group most likely to become pregnant. Of course, pregnancy doesn't stop the bingeing and purging. Rather, the stress of the pregnancy and the bulimic woman's fears of excessive weight gain often exacerbate her eating problems. Professionals who work with bulimics have noticed a high number of miscarriages and birth defects among their clients.

My bulimic clients resemble alcoholics more than they resemble anorexics. Bulimia is alcoholism's sister disease, and by now, alcohol counselors are seeing many women who are both bulimic and alcoholic. Both disorders fit the same general addiction cycle as shown in the diagram.

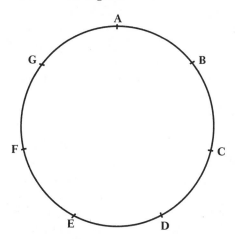

A. The woman loses control of her behavior (she is either drinking excessively or bingeing).

B. She achieves satiety or intoxication, and often sleeps off the effects of her binge.

C. The woman experiences remorse, along with a hangover. Both eating and drinking hangovers include headaches, bad breath, queasiness, irritability of the senses, and exhaustion. At this point, both alcoholics and bulimics feel guilt and shame about their behavior.

D.   The woman vows never to indulge again and feels a temporary optimism that she is back in control.

E.   The stress of ordinary life begins to return and the woman has no coping skills for diffusing the stress. She begins to feel tense and a binge feels appealing.

F.   The woman begins to develop rationalizations for the upcoming bout. For example, "I'll do it just one more time" or "I've proved to myself I can stop, so I might as well celebrate."

G.   The woman decides to stop resisting and eagerly anticipates the reduction in stress that giving in will create.

At any given moment, a bulimic woman is somewhere on the addiction cycle. She is chained to her addiction, a slave to the most primitive and powerful drug of all, food. With an alcoholic, drinking is out of control and with a bulimic, eating is out of control. Alcoholics alternate between abstinence and drunkenness. Bulimics alternate between self-starvation and feeding frenzies. Bulimia, like alcoholism, becomes a way of life. Food in enormous quantities becomes more important than relationships, work, or fun. Just as alcoholics cannot drink moderately, so too bulimics cannot eat moderately.

One of the saddest aspects of bulimia is the victim's inability to eat a normal meal. The women I've worked with can generally eat no more than 400 to 600 calories before they are flooded with anxiety about weight gain. They decide they need to vomit in order to relax about their weight. Since they are going to vomit anyway, they might as well make it worthwhile and binge. This reminds me of the alcoholic who falls off the wagon and says, "Well, I've had one drink so I might as well get plowed." It's all-or-none thinking. One cookie is too many and one hundred cookies are not enough.

An essential part of treatment for drug or alcohol addiction is to stop using the chemicals. An alcoholic resolves never to drink again. He or she avoids former friends who were drinkers and resolves to stay away from bars and other places that feature alcohol. A bulimic cannot stop eating or stay away from food-related activities. She must learn to be a controlled eater. Controlling the drug to which one is addicted is incredibly tough.

I remember a crisis in my work with Cassandra. She was dating a man who wanted to treat her to a luxurious brunch. She wasn't ready to tell him about her bulimia and the idea of brunch was overwhelming. For weeks she made up excuses, but finally she accepted. The morning of the brunch she told him she felt a bit queasy and would only eat lightly. She nibbled on fruit and an unbuttered muffin while her date had platefuls of croissants, pastries, and sausages. Afterwards, she suggested a movie so she wouldn't be able to vomit. Then, at the movie her date bought her a tub of buttered popcorn and a box of mints. She wanted to flee the theater.

The older a habit, the harder it is to break. With both alcoholism and bulimia, early intervention is best. This is difficult as most bulimics are secretive and ashamed of their problem. As with alcoholics, bulimics deny their problems and avoid the reality of addiction. Because they are unable to admit their problem, many bulimics go untreated for years. When they do tell family members, they often find their families confused and uncertain how to help. Other bulimic women who need help simply cannot afford it.

Another powerful aid for alcoholics is the support and encouragement of recovering alcoholics. They can offer sympathy and tips on keeping sober. They can talk tough when the alcoholic is denying or rationalizing away the problem. They know the games. There is even a term, "stinking thinking," for the ruses that addicts employ to avoid facing their problems. When an addict says "I'll quit tomorrow" or blames his or her problem on another person or minimizes the seriousness of the addiction, another addict can recognize the "stinking thinking" from his or her own pretreatment past and confront the person.

Recovering alcoholics can demonstrate to each other that recovery is possible and joyful. They are living proof that there is life after addiction. Unfortunately, few recovered bulimics help their sister victims. Many are willing but they are isolated and quiet about their struggles. Clients ask me, "Does anyone recover from this?"

Alcohol education and treatment help many people stop drinking. Over the years many people have assumed responsibility for educating the young about alcohol, building free and available support groups for alcoholics, and helping the public see alcoholics as needing mental health treatment. Bulimics could benefit from a national effort to help them.

Like alcoholics, bulimics suffer ruined self-esteem and damaged health. Every aspect of their lives is darkened by the addiction. They are adrift, helpless, and set on self-destruct. They need our help. There is a slogan in the alcohol field that I like very much: "The bright side of alcoholism is recovery." Perhaps in a few years, if we can bring it out of the closet, we can say the same thing about bulimia.

The treatment of bulimia is often long-term, complicated, and characterized by many setbacks and crises. I warn women that to recover they must fight the toughest, hardest battle of their lives. Most of my clients struggle for between six months and two years before they are free of the bingeing and purging. Even then, the therapy may not be over, because so much repair work is needed.

Some therapists are unskilled in this area and do more harm than good. Some, for example, prescribe sedatives and tranquilizers that are addictive and only create more problems for the bulimic woman. Other therapists simply have not had experience working with bulimia. They may encourage the client that simply talking about this problem will make it go away. With good therapy, however, most women improve significantly and are eventually symptom-free.

A treatment program should offer the following five components to a bulimic woman: medical care, education and support, planning for a healthy lifestyle, a behavioral program to eliminate bingeing and purging, and therapy to foster insight and attitude change.

Many bulimic women are ill when they seek treatment. Before treatment can proceed, their health must be restored. They need a thorough medical evaluation by a physician familiar with eating disorders. Some women need antidepressants to reduce the intensity of their cravings.

The next step is education. There are many good books available on stress reduction techniques, healthy lifestyles, and fighting addictions. I encourage clients to keep their own journal of observations about cultural attitudes toward women and their bodies. Clients often record analyses of MTV, movies, television shows, and commercials. They may save ads from magazines and record "lookist" comments from others. I encourage women to meet with other women on a weekly basis and talk about their eating disorders.

Healthy lifestyle planning involves learning new behaviors such as exercising three times a week and talking about problems rather than avoiding them. Women also learn time management, stress reduction techniques, and relaxation training.

From the beginning of therapy women keep a journal that includes a record of their eating, the situation at the time, and their feelings. We use this to identify patterns in eating. I encourage women to discriminate hunger from other feelings and act accordingly. Many women binge when tired or bored. With treatment, they learn to sleep when tired and do something interesting when bored. We try to eliminate events that trigger bingeing. Overeaters Anonymous has an acronym that many women find useful: HALT, as in, don't get too Hungry, Angry, Lonely, or Tired.

I recommend three meals and three small snacks a day. These snacks should be high in carbohydrates. Meals should never be skipped. Women must give up their fantasies of losing weight during treatment. A woman cannot diet and conquer an eating disorder at the same time.

I also ask women to bring lunch to my office. While we talk, the client can eat a moderate meal, often one that includes a previously forbidden food. We can discuss her anxiety about eating "so much." She learns that she can eat one cookie and then stop. The rigid eating patterns begin to break up with these lunches.

This procedure worked particularly well with Carla. She'd been unable to eat anything without vomiting. In therapy, she brought a lunch that included some fruit and cheese as well as her beloved fast food. She ate slowly and cheerfully as we talked. Often she rested awhile because she felt too full. When her session was over, she stayed in the waiting room and studied for several hours till her food was digested. Then, she told me with pride that she'd been able to hold everything down.

I discourage television watching because it's prime binge time for bulimics, most of whom are TV watchers. Television offers yet another way to avoid the difficult world of real life. It also promotes junk food, and these ads trigger one impulse to binge after another. Women on television tend to be traditional in their sex roles and slim. These slender, passive sex objects reinforce women's beliefs about their own worthlessness.

Women in therapy contract to meet small but significant

goals for themselves each week. These goals may involve treatment areas, such as reading a book on eating disorders, seeing a doctor for a check-up, exercising, or developing a new interest. Our work together includes a food plan and a commitment to restrict binges to a certain number of times a week. Women must agree not to weigh themselves more often than once a month.

Often I have women draw themselves and bring in these drawings to discuss. The first drawings are tragic. Cassandra came in with a drawing of a big behind and nothing else. Roberta's drawing was of a misshapen torso that was mostly distended stomach. Most bulimic women draw themselves with no facial features. We discuss the drawings as a way to understand their distorted view of themselves. Over time the drawings become more realistic and complete. As the client corrects her view of herself, she begins to draw herself with a face. Later, she might even add a smile or hands that are busy with useful work.

Another important aspect of treatment is having fun. Most bulimics have lost the ability to enjoy anything except bingeing. Because so many bulimics are isolated and withdrawn, I especially encourage fun with others. Acquiring new skills, such as art lessons, writing classes, and athletic or hobby clubs gives women a chance to meet others, keeps the time structured away from food, and builds self-esteem.

In psychotherapy women are encouraged to define themselves in new and positive ways and to regain control of their lives. Women learn to look inside themselves for a sense of direction. Once they know who they are and what they want, they learn to be assertive and ask for those things. All bulimic women need to rebuild destroyed self-esteem. This time their self-confidence will be much sturdier as it will not be based on appearance alone. Much time has been lost during the years of an eating disorder. Therapy helps the women grow again. With hard work, the women can become whole and healthy. They can regain their freedom.

Suggestions for Fighting Bulimia

1. Stop trying to lose weight.

2. Work on eating healthy, ordinary meals.

3. Control eating by learning internal control or by attending a 12-step group that helps you structure your eating.

4. Join a bulimic support group.

5. Have quiet time every day.

6. Talk to someone you trust about your feelings.

7. Fight depression and perfectionism with new kinds of thinking.

8. Raise your consciousness about the way the culture affects your mental health.

9. Develop a wellness program that includes exercise, good nutrition, and stress management.

10. Design new rewards for yourself.

11. Find something to enjoy in every day.

12. Find a good therapist.

CHAPTER EIGHT

Clients with Anorexia

Amanda

On the day of her first appointment, Amanda slouched on my couch dressed in faded blue jeans and a T-shirt that said "Love Sucks." She had a small, pale face and enormous eyes. Her legs curled under her body and she shivered as she answered my questions in a soft, tentative voice.

Yes, she was in drug treatment. Yes, she had used amphetamines for many years to keep her weight down. No, she'd never been in treatment for anorexia. She didn't think she had that problem. She was really fatter than she looked. Yes, she was on a diet and had been on a diet for years. No, she did not eat meals with other people. Yes, her periods had stopped and her hair was falling out. Yes, she had tried to kill herself.

Getting to know Amanda was hard work. She favored monosyllabic answers and was especially reluctant to talk about her feelings, but slowly she shared a little of her past. She had grown up in a wealthy New York family. From the beginning, she was the perfect daughter—beautiful, smart, and compliant. Her father was in real estate and her mother was the archetypal society woman. Amanda was their youngest and favorite child. For her eighth birthday, her parents bought her a beautiful thoroughbred, Countess.

Her dad could be hot-tempered and demanding with other family members, but with Amanda he was relaxed and tender. They rode horses together and Amanda could charm him out of his bad moods. Her mother thought Amanda walked on water.

Amanda had never been spanked and seldom been reprimanded. There was no reason to. She was a straight-A student—and willing to help in any way she could.

When Amanda was 13, her parents separated. Amanda was shocked and confused when her parents sat down with her one night after dinner and told her the news. She listened quietly and even asked what she could do to help them.

She did not share her reactions with them as, "they had enough to cope with at the time." But a few weeks after the announcement she began to diet. She restricted her food intake to 1000 calories a day and started a strenuous exercise program. In three months, she'd lost 30 pounds. She was a bony rack for her size 5 clothes and reported that even a handful of grapes would make her feel full.

Of course, other things changed as well. She lost interest in her old friends, who now seemed immature. She dropped out of 4-H and riding classes. She seemed unable to concentrate on anything and was easily frustrated. She even stopped riding her horse and was indifferent to her father's threats to sell Countess if she didn't ride more often.

She used diet pills to control her appetite. As she grew more weight-obsessed, her grades fell. Her parents were alarmed and considered therapy, but they decided to give her some time. Only when the school called to say she had slit her wrists in the rest room did they seek treatment. Until Amanda was weighed at the treatment center, her parents had not known that she weighed only 92 pounds.

Amanda was like many young women with anorexia. As her world fell apart, she focused on the one thing she could control—her weight. Every day she weighed herself and noted with satisfaction that she was losing more weight. Every night before falling asleep, she would pinch the flesh on her arms, stomach, and thighs and smile as it diminished. Occasionally she remembered that she had once eaten regular meals and ordered banana splits at the nearby Dairy Queen. She couldn't believe that was the same person.

At first Amanda insisted that the divorce and her anorexia were not related. She claimed she understood and accepted the reasons for her parents' divorce. They were happier now and she was happy that they were happy. She denied feeling angry at them.

Well, maybe she was a little angry that they forced her into drug treatment and therapy. But on the other hand, she was grateful to be in treatment and knew her parents had her best interests at heart. Only after some time in therapy did Amanda agree that the divorce and her dieting had started at the same time and that they might be connected.

There were long blue scars on Amanda's wrists from the time she had tried to kill herself. But she had a hard time talking about why she had been suicidal. "I just wanted to go to sleep forever." She could not tell me how she felt about her own life experiences. Her most frequent answer to questions about feelings was, "It was a trip."

After much work, Amanda began to develop greater self-awareness and talk about her real feelings. She stopped mouthing platitudes about her happiness and admitted feeling discouraged, alone, and strange. She thought about who she was, not who she was supposed to be. Since she had spent all of her life trying to please others, this was a tough adjustment. "I don't know what I want or like," she wailed plaintively. "I don't even know how to know."

Then one day she came in and reported that she'd actually had some thoughts of her own. Late Saturday night at the halfway house, she'd discovered that she really liked music from the 1940s. She liked these songs just because she did, not because she should. Having that thought was a breakthrough for Amanda. She realized she had a mind of her own. She began to write down other things she liked and valued, and slowly built a sense of who she was. Brick by brick, she constructed a border between herself and others.

As often happens when people allow themselves to experience their feelings, the first ones that march out are the negative ones. Amanda felt guilty about the divorce and every other failure in the family. Later, she felt angry that her parents had divorced when she desperately needed their help growing up. She was ashamed of her amphetamine use and her failure to stay in school. As she talked about these painful feelings in therapy, she noted with astonishment that for the first time in years she was laughing with her friends.

Soon she began to eat more. She remained frightened of gaining weight, but she brought a sandwich and an apple to my office and nibbled as we talked. At first, this made her extremely anxious. We waited it out. Eventually, Amanda could handle small meals. As she gained weight, she argued and joked with me. Her wooden quality disappeared and was replaced by a lively demeanor. She was on her way to recovery.

Corinna

I first met Corinna in the intensive care unit of a local hospital. She'd overdosed on aspirin and her physician had called me in for a consultation. Corinna was 32 years old but looked about 12. She was so tiny, fragile, and child-like as she lay in the big hospital bed. When I spoke to her, she answered politely and carefully in an almost inaudible voice. Her voice and her body signaled, "I'm small and helpless. Since I won't hurt you, don't attack me."

I continued to visit her in the hospital until she was out of physical danger. After she returned home, Corinna came to my office where, slowly, we explored her situation. She had grown up in a small Oklahoma town, the oldest daughter of an alcoholic father and a frightened, quiet mother. As she put it, "I learned young to keep my mouth shut. What I thought wasn't important. Only what Dad wanted mattered."

Her father tyrannized the house with angry physical outbursts when drunk and with cold, scowling hatred when sober. Her mother scurried about mouse-like, trying to keep herself and the children out of his way. Though frequently beaten, Corinna's mother never filed charges or discussed divorce. Corinna grew up believing that men were tyrants and that women's role was to submit to their brutality.

At 18, Corinna left home and moved to the city to attend computer classes. She enjoyed being on her own, but was frightened by the big city and her new independence. She'd never been in a position to think for herself and make choices about what she wanted and needed. She felt uncertain how to spend her time and money.

She dated almost every night. Several men were interested in her. She found herself nervous about sex and conversation until, during her third month in town, she met Dave. She'd gone to a disco with a friend and Dave had asked her to dance. He told her he was attracted to her vulnerability. Dave was big, brassy, confident, and an alcoholic. In his pushy, macho way, he loved to take care of her. From the beginning they were a couple.

Corinna was in love for the first time in her life. She wanted to be with Dave every minute of her day. She willingly sacrificed her independence for the thrills of togetherness. His drinking bothered her some, but he wasn't a nasty drunk like her father had been.

After four months, Corinna became pregnant. She and Dave were married two days before her 19th birthday. Corinna stayed in school until the twins were born. She dropped out, telling herself she'd go back when the babies were in school.

After a brief honeymoon period, Dave and Corinna's relationship turned into a repeat of her parent's marriage with its poisonous silences, drunken brawls, accusations, and driving-while-intoxicated (DWI) arrests. Corinna accepted this with resignation. She worked full-time, kept the house up, and cared for their twin daughters. She would have stayed married forever, but six years into the marriage Dave moved out. He had found another woman.

Corinna continued to work as a secretary in a large plant. She was an excellent worker, conscientious, uncomplaining, and willing to "help" the bosses in any way she could. She wasn't the kind of politically correct employee who wouldn't make coffee or shop for gifts. She had one sexist and patronizing boss who harassed her continuously, but she put up with him. It didn't occur to her that she had rights in the relationship.

Corinna dated different guys. She was especially popular with alcoholics and found one man after another like her father and Dave. Nice guys didn't appeal to her. Like Groucho Marx, who didn't want to belong to any social club that would have him as a member, Corinna was mistrustful of men who liked her.

She had always seen men as superior to women. Men's thoughts and feelings were the ones that mattered, but men also seemed more childish than women and needed to be humored, flattered, and appeased. She consistently picked men to date that fit this model of reality—dominating, sexist losers who agreed with her that only they were important.

Corinna had never had much of an appetite, and now she grew dangerously thin. She kept her weight under one hundred pounds by rigorous diet and exercise. She liked being small and felt her appearance was her greatest asset. She didn't want any changes that would jeopardize her 20-inch waist and size 7 wardrobe.

Corinna had never had close women friends, since having friends required trusting others enough to share feelings. Corinna didn't trust anybody. Since her image of women was based on her experience of her mother cowering before a brutish husband, she didn't see women as able to stand up for themselves. She didn't even allow herself to feel close to her daughters. She kept them clean and beautifully dressed, but she didn't like to play or snuggle with them.

When she first came in, I asked her about having fun. "Fun," she said. "What's that?" She described herself as never experiencing pleasure. Life was tedious, ritualized, and painful. She was trapped in a gray tapioca world she could not escape.

I encouraged Corinna to take better care of herself at home and work. Since her life had become one long list of tasks to accomplish, Corinna needed to be pushed to do things spontaneously. I encouraged her to do something fun daily. She struggled with this assignment for weeks before she was able to report proudly that she had enjoyed the beauty of a starry night.

Corinna enrolled in an assertiveness class. At first, she was too shy to attend class, but soon she became an enthusiastic pupil. She started taking better care of herself at work. This was difficult, since she had to re-educate all the employees who had taken advantage of "good little Corinna." But with the class and my support, she persevered. Soon she was making friends at work for the first time. She learned that she would get the respect she demanded.

Corinna had spent so many years focusing on others that she didn't really know who she was. In therapy she worked on building a strong sense of self. She kept a daily journal where she recorded her thoughts, feelings, and experiences. I encouraged her to discuss her values and deepest beliefs about people. Sessions began with my asking Corinna, "What did you learn about yourself this week?" She had many answers to that question.

I knew we were progressing when she spoke more warmly about her daughters. She brought in their pictures and talked about the fun she had taking them on a picnic. They had spent a Sunday afternoon under the elm trees in a park along a river. Corinna said she now liked to kiss her daughters' soft faces.

Finally, we focused on her fears of being fat. Corinna was literally afraid to take up much space on the planet. Large meant powerful, and she was terrified of power. All her life she'd been a victim. While being victimized wasn't comfortable, it was familiar. She knew the rules.

As Corinna learned to control some of her world, she relinquished some control of her diet. She stopped weighing herself daily and threw away her calorie charts and diet foods. She was still a small, thin person but she was no longer terrified of gaining weight. She focused on other issues besides her body size.

Currently, Corinna and I are working on her relationships with men. She is committed to breaking her old pattern of seeking and finding losers. I am encouraging her to think about the kind of man she could respect and value and the kind of man who would be a good father to her daughters. Also, I suggested that she be the one to define relationships, rather than be the passive recipient of a man's definition. These ideas are new and frightening for Corinna, but she is tougher than she or I thought. I think she'll make the changes she needs to be a happy and whole person.

Rose

Rose came to see me for follow-up therapy after six months of inpatient treatment for anorexia. By the time I met her, she weighed 100 pounds and had no serious medical problems. But I could tell from reading her records that she had been near death from anorexia. Her weight had been as low as 86 pounds (she was 5 feet, 4 inches tall) and she had been tube-fed when she was first hospitalized.

Since she had wanted to stay in the hospital for another six months, she was not happy to be in my office. Her doctors had pushed her out of the hospital because they felt she was becoming institutionalized. She had made friends on the staff and liked the hospital routines far too much. This forced termination of her treatment made Rose angry.

I was the recipient of her outrage. Our first few sessions consisted of Rose storming that I was incompetent, that she needed to be hospitalized, and that she wanted to work with a male doctor instead of a female therapist "with no medical training." I waited out the storm. When Rose calmed down, she had a more difficult subject to discuss—her life.

Rose was 28 and lived alone in a small apartment. She had always been thin, but her weight became dangerously low after she moved away from home. She had no interest in food and often forgot to buy groceries or cook herself a meal. She had never dated or kissed a man. She knew a few women from her job as a lab technician, but she never really talked to any of them. She never invited anyone to her apartment and reported proudly that her phone rang only once a week, when her parents called on Sunday night.

We discussed her family background which she rather glibly characterized as consisting of "ill health, poverty, and mental instability." Her father was a manic-depressive farmer who supported the family erratically. When he was depressed, he'd found it hard to work. When he was manic, he spent all the family money. Her mother was a long-suffering invalid who loved Rose, but had little energy for rearing a child. Rose grew up on a farm far from town with parents who had no interest in other people. When she left for school, her father's admonishment was, "Now, don't be telling other people our business." She never learned that other people could be a source of nurturance and pleasure. That is, not until she was hospitalized. There, for the first time, she found that people could take care of her—and that it felt good. No wonder she didn't want to leave.

During all those years as an adult living alone, she worked in a laboratory at the same routine tasks. Until she was hospitalized, she had not realized what she was missing. Unfortunately, Rose had no idea of how to find nurturance and support, let alone fun, outside a hospital.

That's what we worked on. I suggested that she had been literally withering away with her anorexia. Her life had just not been satisfying enough for her to want it to continue. We talked about all she had missed—parties, dates, good friends. She had never experienced the carefree joys of childhood or the intense adventures of adolescence. Her adult life had been a wasteland of evenings alone with her television and low-calorie dinners.

The first assignment I gave Rose required her to talk to the other women where she worked, to go out for coffee or a long walk with a colleague. She was uneasy with these tasks, but fortunately, when she tried to make a friend, it worked. Soon she had Molly to visit with every day.

I tried to teach Rose that the world was a warm and interesting place, if she only would trust herself to reach out. She needed to learn about giving and receiving. All of her life she had been too terrified of failure to try many things. Now I tried to help her understand that failure was part of learning and could even be part of the fun. I suggested that every mistake she made socially brought her nearer to her goal of being a regular human being. After a while she reported these failures and sometimes even laughed at her awkward mistakes.

As Rose relaxed about her life, she also relaxed about her weight, which remained low but stable. When she reached 105 pounds, she panicked and insisted that she was now pudgy. We talked about her distorted view of her body. She drew pictures of herself and had Molly take a photo of her in a swimsuit. Gradually, she decided that it was acceptable to weigh as much as 105 pounds.

At first, Rose planned her meals out a month in advance (900 calories each day with absolutely no deviations). She knew how many calories every piece of candy or vegetable contained. But later she allowed herself an occasional spontaneous snack. For example, a co-worker brought a cake for her birthday and Rose had a piece. Later she told me, "I'd forgotten what cake tasted like."

Rose, Corinna, and Amanda all made progress with their anorexia. Though they came from diverse backgrounds and had different life circumstances, all three women had certain things in common when I first met them. All were obsessed with weight and were small and physically weak. More importantly, all had given up on life. They didn't expect to have fun or to find human interaction rewarding.

Their lives had become relentless, grim encounters with scales and calorie charts. Fortunately, this resignation is curable. The most important aspect of their treatment was that they learned that their own thoughts and feelings were valuable and worthy of respect. As they learned that I respected them, they began to respect themselves. When this happened, they grew into fine and complicated human beings.

CHAPTER NINE

Anorexia—Starvation in the Land of Plenty

Once a rare and exotic disease, anorexia is now common. Most women know an anorexic girl or woman or have struggled with the problem themselves. It is estimated that the disease affects between one and six of every two hundred women. Most victims are female and many are between the ages of 12 and 25. Tragically, anorexia is the leading cause of death among people seeking psychiatric help.

Anorexia typically begins with dieting, which may be in response to a crisis or simply at the suggestion of a friend or family member. In its early stages, it looks like normal dieting. Both anorexic and "normal" teenagers fast for days, restrict themselves to only one food, skip meals, and worry unrealistically about their weight.

At first, only a matter of degrees separates the anorexic girl from her peers. She diets harder and insists on being thinner than anyone else. When her friends have stopped dieting, she continues. People tell her that she is too skinny and she likes to hear it. She enjoys pushing herself to lose yet more weight.

Later, the girl develops a certain rigidity in eating habits. She eats only certain foods, prepared in certain ways. She reads diet books religiously and memorizes calorie charts. She compiles mental lists of good and bad foods and follows them to the letter.

Anorexic girls often insist on preparing their own food since no one else can be careful enough. Leanne, an anorexic house guest, insisted on fixing her own meals. She would boil a skinned chicken breast in lemon juice and water, slice it paper thin and wrap it carefully for the refrigerator. Her meals consisted of one slice of chicken on a slice of cucumber. Leanne also had a fondness for frozen packaged diet dinners. They contained carefully measured servings so there was no way she could accidentally overeat.

Anorexic women are often great cooks. They are food-obsessed and love to prepare feasts for friends and family members. Leanne, for example, baked my family an exquisite pineapple cream cheesecake and a delicious French chocolate silk torte. Although she encouraged us to eat and have seconds, Leanne did not sample either of her concoctions.

Leanne spent hours in our kitchen while she dieted. She later received treatment, but during my brief acquaintance with her she was a walking skeleton. She jogged six miles a day and swam laps in the local pool. She reminded me of an inexhaustible particle of energy as she rushed about the kitchen preparing foods she would never taste.

Like all victims of starvation, anorexic females experience a constant gnawing pain in their stomachs, a relentless appetite that cannot be quelled by the tiny snacks they allow themselves. They deny their hunger but they constantly experience overwhelming urges to eat. Their ability to fight down these urges gives anorexic women their limited sense of mastery and control. Sometimes women even test themselves by staying near food but turning it down. Amanda, for example, reported going to pizza parties when she was hungry and not having a bite.

Eventually, anorexic women lose the ability to eat more than small amounts. Many have not eaten a regular meal in years. Even a few bites makes them feel bloated and uncomfortable. I am still surprised when I see the lunches my clients bring. Early on in her therapy, Rose brought a lunch that consisted of three grapes, a Ritz cracker, and two olives. It was her big meal for the day and made her very anxious.

Amanda, my teenage client, is a much more typical case of anorexia than the adult victims, Rose and Corinna. Generally anorexia is a disease of junior-high- and high-school-age girls who do not respond to hunger pangs by eating. Anorexic girls tend to be hyperactive and deny their fatigue.

If the victim of anorexia lives at home, she is likely to be in a power struggle with her parents. They will be alarmed at her weight loss and will attempt, at first gently, to encourage her to eat more. Their cajoling will be futile and their efforts will intensify. There will be scenes around the dinner table with tears, yelling, threats, and bribes. They will fail miserably to stop their daughter's downhill slide into anorexia. Finally, they'll take their daughter, usually over her protests, to a professional.

While teenagers with anorexia are often forced into treatment by their families, adult anorexics may avoid getting help for many years. My clients, Corinna and Rose, are examples of women who were near death before they received treatment for anorexia.

Physical and Psychological Symptoms of Anorexia

As anorexia progresses, serious physical changes are likely to occur. Anorexic women can lose up to 40 percent of their body weight. Starvation makes the body vulnerable to many diseases, and mild infections can be life-threatening to anorexic women. Diarrhea and constipation are chronic problems as the intestinal system grapples unsuccessfully with an inadequate diet. The depletion of protective body fat makes anorexic women vulnerable to hypothermia.

Anorexic women are physically weakened, although their frenetic activity is often mistaken for a sign of good health. Their physical systems are failing. They often stop menstruating. Their hair falls out or gets dry and dull, while their skin becomes rough and red. Ironically, their appearance begins to suffer in many ways. Many indulge in compulsive exercise such as jogging many miles each day. It is heartbreaking to see these women on our streets, training for marathons, as they starve to death.

The psychological changes that come with anorexia are just as devastating. Extroverted girls like Amanda become tense and distant with sullen, pained expressions. Anorexic women's preoccupation with their weight keeps them from focusing on relationships with others. They withdraw further into a ritualized world of diet plans and weigh-ins.

Anorexic women show many of the classic symptoms of depression. Their thoughts are morbid and self-punishing. Nothing seems exciting or fun. Sleep disturbances are common. Life becomes a sort of waking nightmare experienced while numbed with fatigue and obsessed with food.

Anorexics often experience gross disturbances in body image. In one study, anorexic girls were photographed from shoulders down. Later, they were shown photos of their bodies along with the bodies of many other girls of all shapes and sizes. Most could not recognize which body was their own.

This distortion of body image is often accompanied by denial of the anorexia. When family members suggest that they are over-doing their dieting, anorexic girls will deny it. Often they will try to prove they are still fat. Leanne, for example, swore that her upper arms and thighs were flabby. Often girls wear bulky sweaters and tent-like clothes to hide their weight loss. They lie to concerned family members and say they've eaten a meal elsewhere or had a malt after school.

This all-or-nothing approach to dieting is but one example of the black and white thinking that is characteristic of many anorexic girls. This kind of thinking pervades every area of their lives. People either love them or hate them. They are either good or bad. Anorexic girls feel devastated by even the smallest criticism, because they need to be perfect.

When they reach adolescence, most girls find it much harder to be perfect. Life becomes tremendously more complicated. There are so many points of view and divergent opinions about what is right. Anorexics generally feel inadequate and discouraged. They know their system of thinking isn't working. Rather than change systems, however, potentially anorexic girls make serious errors in judgment. They attempt to reduce the complexity of the world to one simple issue—caloric intake.

Like Peter Pan, anorexics tend to view the world of adults with fear and loathing. They don't want to be responsible for their actions and are not ready for independence. They have looked to others for guidance all their lives. They don't know how to make decisions based on their own thinking and feeling.

Like Sleeping Beauty, they await being loved, being brought to life and made worthwhile by the attentions of a man. Their fear of standing on their own two feet is closely related to their need to be validated by a man. In fact, anorexics tend to be popular with men and boys. They are, after all, slim enough and men are attracted to their elfin bodies and child-like behavior. They tend to be great caretakers and listeners. Rather than threatening masculinity, they encourage men to be in control. Pliable and unable to express anger, anorexics will put up with a great deal from a partner without complaining.

Anorexics are masters of self-denial. The smallness of their bodies corresponds to the smallness of their sense of self. Rose, Corinna, and Amanda all had an automaton quality to their behavior. It was as if they were in my office to say and do what they were supposed to do. Sometimes, talking to them, I found myself wanting to say, "Hello, in there! Are you home?"

They had never experienced their own thoughts and feelings as important and worthy of respect. Instead they had learned to constantly scan the environment to see if others were unhappy with them. Corinna had the knack for finding men who agreed with her that only their thoughts and feelings mattered. Amanda had worried too much about pleasing her parents. When they divorced, she had no inner resources to use to help her through the crisis.

Anorexics are driven and obsessed. They feel tremendously guilty about indulgence. Rather like the old Christian martyrs who wore hair shirts and practiced self-flagellation, they feel guilty when they allow themselves pleasure. This inexorable guilt must be discussed and eliminated before the anorexic client can learn to relax and enjoy herself.

What Causes Anorexia?

There are many different theories about how and why anorexia develops. Helen Bruch, who was a pioneer in the treatment of anorexic girls, found that these girls generally came from homes where the parents had imposed an identity on the daughter. That is, the parents had rigid ideas about who their daughter should be and were intolerant of their daughter's shows of independence. Because the girls never developed a sense of self, it was impossible for them to grow up. The developmental hurdles of early adolescence could not be mastered. Adulthood in general, but especially adult sexuality, frightened these anorexic girls. Starving was a way to stay small, asexual, and dependent. Girls could avoid psychological maturity, which requires independent judgments.

Sometimes anorexic girls suffer from a paralyzing sense of ineffectiveness within their own families. They may come from homes where self-expression was not encouraged and mothers tended to be passive and subservient to fathers. In these cases, fathers tended to be preoccupied with achievements and showing off to the outside world. The emphasis was on what other people thought, not what the family members thought or felt.

Salvatore Minuchin, a family systems theorist, sees anorexia as the result of certain family patterns. He has observed that anorexic girls come from families that are intrusive, overprotective, rigid, and unable to deal with conflict effectively. These girls grow up in families that value loyalty and the protection of family members more than autonomy and self-realization. Girls grow up learning to subordinate their needs to those of the family.

Minuchin describes these girls as parent-watchers who take great responsibility for not embarrassing the family. Since anorexics give up on appropriate ways of influencing the world, such as by assertive conversation, they end up with only one way of having power—not eating. With this, an anorexic can say, "I am in control of something. I cannot be made to eat."

Other therapists believe that the anorexic child is the scapegoat for a family with many problems. By starving herself, she manages to keep the focus off more frightening problems in the family such as parental drug use or infidelity.

Cognitive psychologists focus on the disordered thinking of anorexic girls. Eric Button thinks that these girls have developed a view of reality that is too impoverished for them to cope adequately with the complexities of adult life. Like all of us, anorexics need to feel a sense of control and predictability about life. Losing weight means they are safe and good, while gaining weight means they are failures and bad. No ambiguity is tolerated. This impoverished system for assessing reality is too simple to work and fails repeatedly. Their ways of thinking are too simple to allow them to solve the problems they face. Because they keep failing to make sense of the world, anorexics begin to avoid as many real-world situations as they can.

David Epston of New Zealand sees anorexia as a kind of brainwashing. In his analysis, anorexic girls have developed a set of rigid, faulty beliefs about themselves that must be destroyed if they are to recover. They love their worst enemy, anorexia. He feels that therapists must become deprogrammers who encourage girls to argue with that enemy. He and Michael White have formed the Anti-Anorexia League to help girls help each other.

Finally, the sociocultural theory of anorexia suggests that eating disorders are most likely to occur in groups that most value thinness. Rodin found that dancers, a group known to demand extreme thinness, have a notoriously high rate of anorexia. Any population whose living depends primarily on thinness is at high risk.

Glancing at the newspaper corroborates this last point. Brigitte Bardot's ex-husband complained bitterly that she was always on a diet and that there was never any food in the house. Christy Henrich, the gymnast, died in 1994. At the time of her death, she weighed 54 pounds.

Feminists theorize that our culture, with its incessant push for thinness, encourages women to fixate on weight as their one important attribute. Women are valuable if thin and worthless if obese. We should expect eating disorders in a society that teaches this method of evaluating women. In fact, eating disorders are most common among high achievers, those who try hardest to conform to our cultural ideas of perfection.

Treating Anorexia

To a certain extent, therapists use the theories above to determine how to treat their anorexic patients. All of the theories have something to offer. When I work with anorexic clients, I talk about their thoughts, feelings, and behavior, as well as the familial and cultural influences that affect them. Each case is different, and the information these interviews give me helps me decide what kind of treatment or combination of approaches is most appropriate.

What does good treatment involve? Experts disagree on some facets of treatment, but virtually everyone agrees on the first step. Some weight must be restored since it is extremely difficult for a starving person to develop insight and build up self-worth. Since the anorexic may be dehydrated and unable to eat, weight restoration must often be carried out in a hospital. Staffers who work with the patient should be encouraging and supportive at this point because the anorexic woman won't have the energy for psychotherapy until she is healthier.

Once her weight has been restored, psychological treatment can begin. Psychoanalytic treatment involves long-term individual counseling with the emphasis on thoughts and feelings about oneself, one's family, and the therapist. Family systems therapists work with the whole family to change patterns of thought and action. In contrast, a therapist with a cultural bias emphasizes our society's role in creating eating disorders. Typically, he or she encourages the client to question our cultural values regarding attractiveness and to look at our culture with the eyes of an anthropologist. Corrective emotional experiences might be recommended. For example, the girl might be asked to interview someone who is not beautiful, but clearly happy with herself and her life. Or she could interview people from other cultures that are less focused on appearance.

Most forms of treatment require the client to keep careful records of her eating and exercise. Over time a behavioral therapist might suggest small changes in eating behavior. These changes, step by step, will eventually lead to healthier eating patterns.

Most good programs use parts of all the above treatments, tailored to suit the client involved. One issue that arises early is the fear of loss of control over eating. Amanda, for example, was convinced that she was genetically programmed to be overweight. Only by punishing over-control could she hope to avoid weighing 350 pounds. She was afraid that if she relaxed, she would never stop eating. Before Amanda could change, she needed a great deal of reassurance that we could help her control herself and not become dangerously obese.

Treatment must teach the anorexic woman to value herself in new ways. Instead of looking outward for approval, the woman needs to learn that she can be a source of good feelings about herself. These feelings can be based on an appreciation of her own uniqueness, as opposed to her blind conformity to our cultural prescriptions of beauty.

Fortunately, we are making progress in the treatment of anorexia. At one time the death rate was 1 in every 15 girls affected. Now, at some facilities it is as low as 1 percent. Looking at nationwide statistics across several studies, we find that 40 percent of all anorexics recover, 40 percent do quite well but continue to have some problems with eating, and 20 percent make no significant progress.

The Influence of Culture

At one time, I thought that family systems theories were the most useful ways to look at anorexia. At this point, however, I've seen more and more anorexic girls coming from normal, stable homes—and I think the cultural theories may be more important. These cultural theories seem to best explain the enormous rise in the incidence rates of anorexia.

Of course, within our culture some women are more vulnerable than others. Passive girls and girls raised in appearance-oriented families are definitely more vulnerable. Girls who have been subjected to a steady diet of mass media—with all its dangerous messages contained therein—are also more at risk than girls who spend their time developing their own talents.

In the past, I think we mental health professionals have been terribly remiss in ignoring these cultural influences. As a result, we have treated each individual woman as if she were the only victim of an eating disorder, or we have encouraged women to see themselves and their families as the culprits.

We have done this because, like most people, psychologists feel unable to change culture. It is much easier to try to change an individual. However, by ignoring cultural forces, we have focused on treating casualties, not preventing victims. As the number of victims rises, we need to change our focus. Too many women have learned to blame themselves. By focusing on the cultural factors, we can bring anorexic woman back from their isolation, and help them feel more comfortable seeking help and helping others.

As we learn from our clients, our treatments will become better and more sophisticated. But we also need to work toward the changes necessary to prevent this sad disease. At present, we can try to design effective treatments for the young women who have been infected with anorexia through our mass culture. But it is better to inoculate our young women against this cultural disease.

Tips for Women Struggling with Anorexia

1. Find a good therapist and a doctor experienced in dealing with the medical problems of anorexic women. Self-help books cannot substitute for professional help with anorexia.

2. Don't diet, skip meals, or weigh yourself. Avoid diet books and calorie counting. Avoid magazines, TV shows, or exercise classes that focus on the importance of being thin.

3. Join a support group for anorexics. You'll find good advice, experience, and support.

4. Set reasonable limits on your exercise. If you are a dancer, gymnast, athlete, or otherwise depend on staying thin as part of your livelihood, pay special attention to maintaining healthy eating habits.

5. Keep track of your tendency toward perfectionism. Look for opportunities to be less strict or judgmental with yourself. It's okay to make mistakes.

6. Don't let your weight and appearance be the central issues in your life. Find a cause to believe in, or a hobby or activity to be involved in. The more you are able to cultivate other interests, the better you will feel about yourself and the less you will be able to focus on not eating.

7. Learn to process your pain and talk about your feelings. Learning to identify and value your own thoughts, feelings, and goals will help you overcome the self-effacing attitude that characterizes anorexics.

8. Learn to be more assertive in meeting your own needs. There's a big difference between self-care and self-ish. Assertiveness training or even public speaking courses can help you learn to let others know what you think and what you need.

9. Keep a journal of how you feel about yourself, your eating behaviors, and everyday events. Use it to learn to develop your own thoughts and feelings rather than depending on others.

10. Start valuing yourself for attributes other than appearance. Keep a list of your successes and achievements—no matter how small they seem at the time.

CHAPTER TEN

Obese Clients

Florence

Florence was the red-headed youngest child of a Missouri farm family with three older sons. As a girl, Florence was energetic, curious, and outgoing. But almost overnight, when she was 11, Florence's personality changed. She stopped laughing and joking and withdrew deep into herself. She lost interest in school and social life and instead spent all her time watching television or shadowing her mother as she did the chores.

Florence ate nonstop. She ate at meals, between meals, and before meals. She sneaked cookies and crackers into bed with her. In the span of a year she went from being stocky, but healthy, to being obese. Her parents noted the changes, but they were unsophisticated people and had no idea what to do. They asked the minister to talk to Florence. He asked her what was wrong, but she was too shy to tell him. They prayed together and then Florence went home to her sad, self-destructive eating.

Florence became quieter and quieter. She had trouble sleeping and often would walk up and down the hallways all night long. She spent less and less time with friends and eventually they quit asking her to do things. All through junior high school, Florence gained weight. By high school, she needed special clothing and size 3 FFFF shoes. She had trouble exercising and was winded and tired from even the smallest exertion.

Needless to say, her high school years were excruciating. All the girls began dating. She went to one dance and never tried again. The boys had mocked her pitilessly. She tried dieting, but would become immediately depressed. Even the mention of weight caused her to burst into tears. Food was solace in her isolated and difficult world. Earlier she had clung to her mother, but by now she was angry that her mother didn't understand and help her. So she turned away from her as well. She hardly spoke to her father and her brothers.

After high school, Florence looked for work in St. Louis. In spite of the fact that she was a good worker, the only job available to her was janitorial work in an office building. The pay was minimum wage and it made her tired and achy. Twice she sprained her back. But Florence plugged away at the boring menial work. She had no choices.

She didn't make friends in the city, but she didn't miss her family. She never called home. She spent most of her time off watching her small television. Saturday nights she ordered a large pizza delivered and watched movies on the cable channel.

Her weight bothered her. She had lost interest in how she looked, but she was in pain from arthritis and lower back troubles. She was afraid she wouldn't be able to work. Finally, she grew desperate enough to seek a stomach stapling operation. She was terrified of surgery, but was willing to risk her life to lose weight. She said tearfully, "I'll do anything to lose weight."

After some testing and counseling, Florence was admitted to the hospital for surgery. She almost died on the table. Her heart stopped twice and her blood pressure plummeted. Afterwards she was in intensive care for a week. She was in too much pain to speak, but stared at her visitors across all the modern gadgetry with shocked, betrayed eyes. A tube as thick as a pencil was inserted in her mouth and intravenous needles poked into both arms.

For several weeks Florence remained in the hospital and could only sip clear liquids through a straw. By six weeks, her system could handle mouthfuls of broth and she was sent home. For several more weeks, Florence was in pain and could barely walk from her bed to the bath. She had lost fifty pounds, but was too sick to care.

As soon as she was well enough to eat solid foods, Florence stopped losing weight. Her stomach was now so small that she would often be sick after eating a meal. But she didn't stop eating. She developed a bulimic eating pattern and gained back all the weight she lost, plus more. She now weighs over three hundred pounds and has a moon-shaped scar across her abdomen.

I met Florence when her company's employee assistance program encouraged her to set up an interview. She sat in my office, hands folded across her lap, with big sad eyes filled with tears. That first session she told me of her life. I was struck by how flat her voice was when she talked about her family. For the day, I let that pass. Instead I tried to listen respectfully and praise her good choices, such as coming to therapy. Some time later, I asked her about her brothers. She sighed and looked hard into my face. I said softly, "You can tell me."

That day was the beginning of Florence's attempt to process her pain. Earlier she had tried to avoid her feelings by eating. The feeling of satiety kept her sadness at bay. Now she talked about what had actually happened to her. She spoke with reluctance, but also with courage about her sexual experiences with her brothers. She cried quietly as she talked. When she finished, I thanked her for telling me the painful truth. I said, "Now you will begin to heal."

Florence continued to come in. She didn't make much progress with her bulimia, partly because of the physical problems she had acquired with the surgery. She never lost weight and resisted mightily my efforts to build an exercise program into her life. But as she talked about her difficult years at home, she felt better at times. She smiled and even laughed.

The best thing she did was to get a collie puppy. Her involvement with that dog changed her life. She brought me pictures of "Mister" and she bought herself collie paraphernalia—buttons, postcards, even a sweatshirt. Now she had someone to go home to each night, someone who was desperately eager to see her. She had a reason to get out of bed in the morning. Mister needed to be let out. Occasionally, she even took a walk and visited with people curious about Mister. Dogs, like babies, are great conversation starters. When I wanted to cheer Florence up, I asked her about Mister. That always brought a smile.

Gina

Gina's complaint, when she first sat nervously in my office, was that she needed to lose weight. In the five years since her divorce, she had gained 50 pounds and now weighed over 200 pounds. She said she hated her fat and desperately wanted to change.

Gina had china doll features and a porcelain complexion, but she clearly didn't try to make much of her appearance. She dressed in dowdy grays and browns and her hairstyle was severe. She wore no makeup.

Even though Gina claimed she wanted to lose weight, her behavior suggested the opposite. She had joined an exercise spa, but had only been there once in six months. She had not dieted and, in fact, kept M&Ms and pecan cookies in her locker at work. At home, her freezer was filled with ice cream and pastries.

Gina was a nurse supervisor at a local hospital. She worked long and irregular hours at a high-stress job. The staff kept the nursing station filled with donuts, cookies, and pies. She was a big sister to the other nurses and helped them with their problems on and off the job. She also cared for the doctors and had a reputation for being the best nurse in the hospital. If something needed to be done, Gina would do it, no matter how inconvenient or difficult it was for her. Of course, the patients loved her. Gina was great at taking care of other people.

She was also the caretaker in her family. Her parents were ill and poor. They could count on Gina for money when they needed it and also for nursing care. After her long shifts at work, Gina would stop by their place to see if she could help them in any way. Gina was the one who held the family dinners on the holidays, remembered the nieces and nephews with checks on their birthdays, and helped everyone with their taxes. No matter if people didn't remember her birthday.

As we talked, it became clear that Gina was a caretaker in every relationship she had. Her way of being was to give, and she had no concept of a mutual relationship. She even gravitated toward needy friends whom she could nurture.

This had definitely been the situation with her marriage. She had married an insecure man who had grown increasingly dependent on Gina. By the time they had divorced, Gina was earning the living, doing all the housework, and being emotionally supportive of her depressed husband. Surprisingly, he had left her. His therapist, whom Gina had paid, advised him that Gina was not good for his mental health.

Given her history, it made sense that Gina would be frightened of another relationship. To be in a relationship was to give her all and expect nothing in return. As we talked about this, Gina admitted she did not want to lose weight. Because if she did, men might ask her out. If she dated, it was just a matter of time until she found another dependent man to care for. She no longer had the energy.

When I suggested that Gina could learn to be in a relationship as an equal, not a nurse, and that she could take care of herself and demand respect, Gina was skeptical. We started with relationships at the hospital. I encouraged Gina to set some limits. She, like other employees, could refuse requests to work overtime, second shifts, and holidays. She could ask other nurses to do more of the work so that she was not chronically exhausted on the job. She could even say "no" to the doctors.

At first, Gina found this difficult. She feared rejection every time she set a limit or denied a request. But Gina wasn't rejected, and she learned that people liked her even if she cared for herself. Soon she was enjoying work and reported, with some surprise, that she seemed to be more valuable as an employee now that she was in control of her life at the hospital.

Next we tackled her relationships with her family and friends. These were harder to change. For one thing, everyone was spoiled and resisted Gina's attempts to care for herself. Her parents accused her of not caring for them. Her siblings were reluctant to share the burdens: "You have done such a good job, and we are so busy." But, with my support, Gina persisted. She cared for her family, but not all by herself and not all the time. She divided up holiday dinner chores among all the siblings. When her parents needed financial help, she called in everyone to deal with the problems.

We discussed her friendships. Her friends were a needy bunch who depended on Gina for advice, rides, and other forms of attention. When she had needs, however, they were unavailable. I suggested it was time to make new friends. Slowly, Gina learned how she could structure relationships so that she was doing only 50 percent of the giving. She learned to ask for help from others. To her surprise, people were willing to give it to her.

We discussed her fears of dating. Intimacy for her meant being swallowed up by another's needs. Anyone would be afraid of that. I suggested that until she felt strong enough to care for herself in a relationship, she would avoid losing weight. We talked about how she could define relationships so that she could be in control at least half the time and her needs could be met.

About six months into her therapy, the lab manager at the hospital asked her out to dinner and a movie. Gina decided to go. They had a good time and together they planned another date, this time to a nearby state park to go fishing. Fortunately, George was a healthy person who was quite content with equal relationships. When Gina found the courage to assert herself, he was responsive. Sometimes, he cooked her meals and soon he was working on her car and helping her rewallpaper a room in her house. With his help, she learned that mutual relationships were possible and lots of fun.

Over time, Gina's clothing became brighter and less baggy. She let her hair grow into a softer, prettier style. Without ever discussing her weight, she began to exercise. Gradually her body firmed up and she even lost a little weight. She reported loving to swim and play racquetball. She also stopped gorging on sweets at work and at home. She had learned in her relationship with George that closeness didn't mean being a doormat. Because she felt in control of her relationships for the first time in her life, she could risk being attractive.

Amy

During her senior year in high school, Amy asked her parents if she could see a counselor. She came eagerly to my office to discuss her feelings about her body. Bright and articulate, Amy was a delightful client. She dressed in the latest teen fashions and was in many ways poised and confident. She weighed over two hundred pounds.

When Amy was adopted as a baby, she was exceptionally chubby. Her obesity was most probably genetic. Her biological mother had been heavy. Her adoptive parents were thin and wiry, and her sister was positively petite. Amy had good eating habits and had avoided the diet trap. She loved to exercise and had been a tennis player since she was 11. But she was fat and had no reason to hope that would ever change for her.

In kindergarten, she had needed special-order "chubby girl" clothing. In second grade, she had broken a chair in the music room and felt she would die from the embarrassment. Her memories of grade school were colored by taunts and jokes about her weight. She had learned to hide the pain and even joke about herself. "Kids liked me," she said. "But they didn't know how much they were hurting me."

Junior high school had been the worst. In addition to her weight gains, she'd had acne and greasy hair. She said, "I could hardly bear to walk past boys in the halls. I knew what they were thinking about me." Amy shuddered when she told me about showers. As she hauled her flabby body in and out of the crowded shower stall, she would hear girls as slim as models complain about invisible bulges on their calves and thighs. In fact, she had stayed home sick whenever she could.

Of course, Amy did not date. Everyone, including the boys, liked her for a friend, but no boy was brave enough to date a fat girl. She hated Saturday nights, spent alone at her house, while her petite sister and friends were at the movies with one attractive boy after another.

By the time she got to high school, she was accustomed to the pain. She grew familiar with rejection and learned to compensate. Her grades were outstanding and she was a member of the tennis team. Because she was smart and friendly, she had lots of friends, at least until Saturday night.

Amy was lucky in that her parents felt she was great at any size. Her sister was proud of her accomplishments. She was as well-adjusted as a heavy girl could be. However, she came to me almost as a victim of post-traumatic stress. This is a diagnostic term for the suffering faced after the fact by victims of stressful events such as the Vietnam War or earthquakes. Victims of severe stress must talk about the stress or they are likely to have psychological problems. Amy instinctively knew this. She had so much pain, and she didn't want to burden her loving family. She needed some place where she could be honest and not worry about hurting the listener.

So I listened. I listened while she talked about the teasing, the jokes, the smart cracks, the inadvertent comments that had cut to the bone. I listened while she struggled to define herself as special and important in spite of years of being treated as defective and inferior. I listened as she cried, reviewing one lonely and isolating experience after another. There was an avalanche of pain that needed to be dealt with and sifted through. For many years, Amy had been quiet and a good sport. Meanwhile, the damage was being done.

I did what I think good therapists do when clients talk about trauma. It's called "being and staying." I asked questions, listened respectfully, and handed her tissues when she cried. I felt impotent as I listened. I could reinforce her sense of injustice and I could praise her adaptability in the face of such problems. I could encourage an assertive approach with the most insensitive of her tormentors and I could underscore her many strengths and skills. But, in the end, I couldn't give her enough. She left therapy relieved to have found a confidante, but she returned to a world where large women are discounted and scorned.

Will Amy be able to marry the man of her choice? Will she be able to secure the job she wants? I cannot promise her any of these happy endings. Unless our attitudes about women change dramatically, I can only listen as she works through her pain. Amy—with Gina and Florence and all of the other large women who suffer from our society's intolerance—deserve a better, more compassionate world that appreciates them for who they are.

CHAPTER ELEVEN

Obesity—Being Fat in America

A former client recalled an incident that took place when she was 19. Delores and her fiancé were at a ballroom, spinning about on the polished hardwood dance floor. The band played a waltz and then the "Beer Barrel Polka." When the band finally took a break, Delores and her partner returned to their table for a cool drink. As they relaxed, Delores overheard the man at the next table say, "I'm glad she's off the floor. Her fat butt was ruining the atmosphere."

Delores gasped, unable to believe what she had heard, but a look at her partner's miserable face confirmed her fears. She asked to go home. Twenty years later she could hardly tell me the story, because she was still so hurt and embarrassed by the thoughtless man's remarks. She's never been dancing again.

Gina returned from a family Christmas and told me of an incident with her brother. The two of them had gone out to coffee to talk about their work. He complained that a good secretary was hard to find. He mentioned that a well-qualified, obese woman had applied. "But I could never hire anyone who's fat," he said. "Why, even someone as fat as you would cause me to lose customers."

Amy and Florence have both told me of painful incidents from their high school days. Florence recalled boys making bets on football games. The boy whose team lost would have to walk her to class. Amy remembered going to her first dance and watching boys accept money in exchange for dancing with her. Red-faced and trembling at the memory, she said, "That's when I learned to hate."

While these examples may sound extreme, they are not

uncommon. Most obese women have heard remarks like the ones quoted above. They've experienced fat lady jokes, stares, and ridicule. They have learned to feel anxious and defensive about their bodies.

Even their physicians and therapists may have attacked them, "for their own good." Many women have been lectured by their doctors. They were accused of lying, stuffing themselves, and being stubborn. Others have gone into therapy, only to find their therapist as openly condemning of fat as their worst enemy.

Who has the power to label these women obese? Hollywood? Our families? Our doctor? Value-laden terms such as *overweight*, *fat*, and *obese*, roll off our lips glibly and with great certainty. We may not know how to define fat, but we know it when we see it.

Definitions of obesity vary some from group to group. Many high school girls think anyone heavier than Brooke Shields or Diana Ross is overweight. The fashion industry with its emaciated models suggests that 95 percent of all women are overweight. Older rural women have a very different idea. In general, men face a less exacting standard of thinness than women.

Most people would trust their doctor's evaluation. Unfortunately, doctors can be just as biased and fat-phobic as anyone else. They often react on the basis of their own personal standards as opposed to solid data about obesity. Furthermore, even their standard height-weight charts, which they tend to use in formulating their professional opinions, are subjective.

There is nothing very scientific about these charts. They aren't based on medical evidence and there is no compelling reason to believe that people above their desirable weights are any less healthy than others. The original tables were designed by a biologist who worked for an insurance company. He published the first "ideal weights" during the 1940s and led a vigorous national campaign against obesity. He first promulgated the now-widespread belief that thin people are healthier.

His versions of the tables were based on many false assumptions. For example, one of his assumptions was that adults shouldn't gain weight after age 25. We now know that a healthy person's weight normally rises a bit with age. He also assumed that people could be accurately assigned to one of three frame sizes— light, medium, or large. With all of today's medical and technological sophistication, we still do not have a reliable way of determining the correct frame size for an individual.

These early ideas about the relationship between thinness and health have since been discredited. For example, since 1948, life expectancy data has been collected as part of a study of the residents of Framingham, Massachusetts. During the 1980s, doctors analyzed this data to examine the relationship between longevity and weight. Among women the death rate was highest in the lightest and heaviest groups. For the majority of women, those whose weight fell between these two extreme groups, there was no relationship at all between weight and mortality. The doctors concluded that, in terms of longevity, the best weight was probably somewhat above the average for both men and women.

For another study, Dr. John Andres of Johns Hopkins University analyzed weight-health data over a 14-year period. He found that the lowest mortality occurs in adults who would normally be considered 24 to 38 percent overweight. All this suggests that, for the vast majority of weight-conscious women or men, being thin is a cosmetic—not medical—necessity.

The Obese Personality

At one time psychologists assumed that people who were heavy had deep-seated psychological problems—and that their psychological problems caused their obesity. Now we realize that obesity creates stress reactions in its victims. Many obese women exhibit a constellation of traits psychologists have identified as traits of victimization. That is, they have many traits that are the result of their continual experience of being maligned and rejected by others. These include low self-esteem, high social anxiety, a tendency to avoid crowds, feelings of estrangement from others, and depression.

These women also suffer because of their attempts to lose weight. Because many of them diet continuously, they come to resemble other starving populations. Starvation induces depression, irritability, and sluggishness. Being hungry leads to a constant preoccupation with food.

There is evidence that heavy women in less fat-phobic cultures do not suffer special psychological or physical problems. They neither diet nor feel persecuted. If heavy women felt comfortable with themselves and did not diet, would they still suffer from high blood pressure? We know, for example, that blacks have higher blood pressures in racist than nonracist cultures.

Stress is certainly a factor in hypertension. Perhaps what has been most dangerous to heavy American women is that their self-loathing catapults them into such a host of self-destructive behaviors. Obese people, as a group, are as healthy emotionally as other groups, except for the problems caused by reactions to their size.

Dieting Is Not the Answer

Obesity has been associated with high blood pressure and adult diabetes. However, even if obesity is a risk factor for some diseases, dieting is not necessarily the answer. Radical diets are often more dangerous than the obesity they are trying to correct. Research has shown that the heart is stressed by a weight loss or weight gain of more than 10 pounds. Heavy dieting can also lead to arteriosclerosis, which increases the risk of strokes and heart disease. Refeeding, or normal eating after heavy dieting, can produce marked irregular heartbeats and cause sudden death.

Many of the habits gained while dieting are also self-destructive. Many girls and women develop an addiction to methamphetamine while dieting. Teenage girls use tobacco as a hunger suppressant. Many girls smoke because they are afraid they will gain weight if they stop. And diets lead to aberrant eating patterns that make women vulnerable to the development of eating disorders.

Finally, dieting is not a good solution because it doesn't work. Ninety percent of all dieters regain their weight. Health problems can be addressed by other solutions besides dieting. For example, women can successfully learn to restrict their sodium intake. Stress management techniques can reduce high blood pressure and exercise can improve health in a variety of ways.

The Causes of Obesity

Let's look at some of the possible causes of obesity. Medical theories of obesity now include the fat cell theory, biochemical theories, genetic theories, and insulin-related theories.

First of all, "large" is one of the many natural sizes of the human species. Human body size, like most other traits, follows a bell-shaped curve pattern of distribution. In a normal population, intelligence is distributed in this same pattern. Some people will be brilliant, while others will be slow learners. Most of us will fall somewhere in between. Likewise, in a normal population, some perfectly healthy people will be large, some will be small, and most will be in the middle.

A recent study by A. J. Stunkard involving more than five hundred adoptive children and both their biological and adoptive parents showed decisively that the genetic factor is all-important. The adopted children and their biological parents were closely correlated in weight. There was no relationship at all between the weights of children and their adoptive parents.

A unique physical condition can predispose a woman to a large size. Some medical problems such as glandular and metabolic disturbances can lead to obesity. Deep-seated psychological problems can also contribute to obesity. Depression and certain psychotic states may lead to overeating and a lack of exercise. Misuse of food can lead to obesity. Susie Orbach, author of *Fat Is a Feminist Issue*, wrote about compulsive eaters who used food to deal with all of life's problems. She distinguished "mouth hungry" from "stomach hungry." Certainly, eating to meet psychological needs can contribute to obesity.

Dieting is also a common cause of obesity. The more women diet, the more obese they become. Binges, for example, are a natural reaction to chronic food deprivation. Dieting turns the woman into an externally controlled eater. Furthermore, a woman's "set point" is likely to rise in response to dieting. Her system is damaged and no longer functions in a healthy, adaptive manner.

Probably the most common reason that people are considered overweight today is our culture's narrow definition of appropriate weight. Teenaged girls, raised with Barbie, describe the ideal height and weight as 5 feet 7 inches and 110 pounds. Since the beginning of the century, attractiveness has been defined in thinner and thinner terms. Women that would have been called "skinny Minnies" and put on weight-gain diets a few years ago are now just right or even too heavy. Just as having a 55-mile-per-hour speed limit made many of us speeders, promoting the very thin as the norm has made most of us overweight.

Growing Up Fat-Phobic

Women learn about our cultural intolerance for fat when they are very young. Pudginess is cute in toddlers but it grows less attractive with each passing year. By the time a child starts kindergarten, chubbiness is penalized. Even kindergartners have internalized our cultural norms about ideal body size. By age five, children constantly select pictures of slender bodies and reject rounded ones when asked to identify good-looking people.

School-age children of both sexes have been shown to have more negative attitudes toward the obese than toward bullies, the handicapped, or children of different races. We teach our children to hate and fear what we hate and fear. One study found that school children attributed the following traits to obese children: "lazy, sloppy, mean, dirty, cheats, and arguers." Even as a child, to be overweight means to be condemned by one's peers for a host of stereotyped personality characteristics.

Overweight children are harassed mercilessly and are generally the last chosen for games, even those of a nonphysical nature. We all remember the childish words for taunting the obese—fatso, fatty, piggy, and big, fat slob. At the elementary school level, heavy children are shunned. Twenty years later, when I see these grown-up children in therapy, they are still in pain from this abuse.

A vicious cycle comes into play. Because an overweight girl is isolated and rejected, she is more likely to need comforting and to take comfort in food. She is less likely to be asked to play active games and more likely to refuse because of her embarrassment about her body. So she grows even more obese and isolated.

Most adults do little to mitigate this destructive process. Parents sometimes aid in the victimization of their own children. Once when I was shopping, I overheard a mother talking to her daughter, who was trying on party dresses. She put on each dress and then asked her mother how she looked. Time after time, her mother responded by saying, "You look just awful in that, Kathy. You're so fat that nothing fits you right." The mother's voice dripped with disgust and soon Kathy was crying. "Oh, why won't you lose weight?" the mother shouted in angry despair.

Kathy will never forget the lesson she learned that day in the dressing room. Yet her mother is a victim, too. She knows what a tough world it is for chubby women. No doubt she has tried to help Kathy lose weight and repeatedly experienced failure. She is as helpless as Kathy to change the situation that will make her daughter's future life difficult. Sadly, Kathy's weight has even affected the quality of their mother-daughter relationship.

Pressure from parents to be thin does damage parent-child relationships. Ambitious fathers sometimes use emotional blackmail to shape up their daughters. I've heard of fathers bribing daughters with new cars or trips to Europe if they will only lose weight. One college student client told me, "My dad says it embarrasses him to be seen with me at his club when I'm overweight. He'll only take me when I'm thin." I have one friend who never goes home. "All my mother cares about is how much I weigh," she says bitterly.

The High Cost of Being Heavy

Being obese produces enormous shame in most women. Is it any wonder? We are bombarded by messages stating that obese women are disgusting. For instance, a bumper sticker I've seen recently says, "Save the whales/Harpoon a fat lady." I've also seen a sticker that shows the universal symbol for "no" over the words "No fat chicks." We have all heard good, and in many ways sensitive, people say things like, "I can't help it, I just find fat women disgusting."

One client said the image she saw when she heard the word "obese" was of a lower-class woman in a soiled housecoat eating sugar donuts in a trailer full of wailing kids. We all have negative associations to the word obese—gross, fat, slob, disgusting, slut, lazy, stupid, dirty, slovenly, poor, or wallowing.

Society's rejection of the obese is unusually thorough. Generally, most of us can separate an alcoholic's behavior from his or her personhood. Smokers may find their behavior is criticized, but they are still valued as people. Obese people are condemned not just for their overeating (a behavior that is not necessarily present). Their entire character—from their IQ to their work habits and their sexuality—is imagined, judged, and found wanting.

The obese learn to avoid situations where they might be teased or traumatized. They stay away from beaches, sport courts, and other areas where scanty clothes are necessary. They avoid dancing, athletics, and public dining because, as Delores put it, "it disgusts others to see me stuff my face." As Susie Orbach says, "To be fat is to be excluded from contemporary mass culture, from fashion, sports, and outdoor life."

Obese women are often their own harshest critics. They feel repulsive, guilty, and ashamed of their appetites. They have tried to change, but they have failed and blame that failure on themselves. Many do not realize that the game is rigged, and they are the losers.

Some women even use the culture's loathing to motivate themselves. I saw an ad recently for an "oinkalator." It's an alarm that goes "Oink, Oink" when the refrigerator is opened. One woman told me that her weight-control group had a pig pen where members who had gained weight had to stand during meetings. These women are deliberately internalizing our culture's fat-phobia.

Thin people reap social and political rewards. The fat become outcasts. As our culture's increasingly radical definition of thinness becomes harder to achieve, more of us will fall into this outcast class. Many women are desperate, and desperate people are easy prey for marketers. Just as cancer patients will spend an exorbitant amount of money on unproven treatments, women frightened of being heavy will spend money and risk their health on all kinds of gimmickry.

Other women see the exclusion of their overweight sisters and are warned to stay thin, or they too will suffer like these pariahs. It is no wonder I see clients who say they would rather kill themselves than be overweight. Fat is the leprosy of the 1990s.

Why Do People Hate Fat?

Where does this hatred of fat originate? Some psychoanalytic theorists postulate that it is the fear of the all-powerful mother. When we are small, our mothers can overwhelm us with their size. We all have intense feelings that remain from the time when we were helpless and our mothers were the all-powerful controllers of our lives. As we grow up, this anger may be expressed by lashing out at maternal-looking or large women.

Other theorists emphasize that a hatred of fat is a thinly disguised hatred of female sexuality. After all, female sexuality is flesh, roundness, softness, and curves. Obese women may trigger fears of sexuality run amok or passion unbridled by civilized restraints. By raging at obese women, the sex-phobic's fears are quieted.

Feminists associate our nation's growing fat phobia with the steady rise in power of women in our culture. The other time during this century when thin women were the ideals was the flapper era, also an era of expanded political rights for women. In the late 1950s, when women's political power was at a low ebb, Marilyn Monroe, with all of her voluptuous curves, was our cultural ideal of feminine pulchritude. Since that time our ideal has become slimmer, more angular, and boyish. Feminists suggest that to counterbalance the threat of formidable real women, our culture has defined the ideal woman as weaker and smaller. Models now look hungry, wan, and weak as kittens.

In fact, women obsessed with becoming thin do not have much time to worry about becoming rich or powerful. "Diet, don't riot" has become our culture's extraordinarily effective message to women. Most of us worry more about our weight than our wages. We expend more energy on our appearance than on our empowerment. Certainly women spend more time and energy controlling their weight than on changing the political structure of the country.

Fighting Back

Many people believe that fat women get what they deserve. "After all, it's their own fault if they're overweight. They just need willpower like the rest of us." For a long time this overt discrimination against the obese went unchallenged. But over the past decade, women have begun to question the fairness of these messages to and about the obese. Women have begun to analyze the media and its effects on their self-esteem. They boycott products that advertise in ways that are demeaning to women. Some have canceled their subscriptions to women-hurting magazines.

These women have called for a new understanding of our cultural attitudes toward weight. They have asserted that biology, not eating habits, is the main cause of obesity. They cite research that indicates that the health problems of the obese are not due to weight but to stress, self-hatred, and chronic dieting. They encourage obese people to accept themselves as they are and not wait to be thin to live.

In the 1980s, a civil rights movement for the obese was born. Books sharing the rage and pain of the obese were published. My favorite was *Shadow on a Tightrope*, edited by Lisa Schoenfielder and Barb Weiser. Movies, such as *Fat Chance in a Thin World*, protested the injustice of fat phobia and sensitized viewers to how it feels to be obese. *Radiance: A Publication for Large Women* accepted only ads and articles that respected and affirmed large women.

In the 1990s this movement is still small, but growing. Women are helping each other accept and value their bodies, whatever their shapes and sizes. Hopefully, by the end of this decade, our culture's stereotyping of and discrimination against the obese will be history. Our daughters will not have to suffer and see their friends suffer. They will look back on this time in disbelief, as we do when we think of our grandmothers not being able to vote or own property. They will be grateful for our efforts at changing the world in which they live.

Suggestions for Large Women

1. Develop a wellness program for yourself that includes good nutrition, exercise, and stress management.

2. Throw away your scales. Accept yourself as you are right now.

3. Learn new ways to reward and treat yourself that are not food-related.

4. Buy attractive clothes that are comfortable and fit properly.

5. Find a doctor who is nonjudgmental and sympathetic.

6. Write and memorize self-affirmations that you can recite when you are tempted to judge yourself harshly. Start each day with a quiet moment of contemplation.

7. Form or join a support group for large women.

8. Fight lookism and stereotypes about large people in yourself and in others. Keep in mind all of your—and other large people's—good qualities. Let these qualities define you, not your dress size.

9. Write and boycott businesses and media that belittle the obese.

10. Pursue your dreams now. Do not wait until that mythical day when you are thin.

CHAPTER TWELVE

Feeling Good

"I was 35 before I ever exercised. Well, I take that back. I lifted a coffee cup or a cigarette to my lips hundreds of times a day. I was always tired and mentally sluggish. I was mildly depressed. On my birthday I noticed flab on my arms and realized my body was aging rapidly. I signed up for a water aerobics course. I loved it from the beginning. I immediately felt more alive. I can't believe I went 35 years without moving. Now if I don't go for a day, I miss it."

JANE, IN THERAPY

This chapter is written for women who are coping with the normal weight and body image problems that most American women encounter. It summarizes the common mistakes women make that may lead them to misuse food and feel badly about themselves. It also reviews many of the suggestions I've made in earlier chapters for changing eating behaviors and lifestyle. Finally, I will pass along the inspirational story of a woman with a healthy lifestyle and a good attitude toward food and her body.

Women who are currently fighting an eating disorder need more support and guidance than this chapter offers. I recommend that they seek therapy with someone experienced in treating them. Group therapy with other women with similar problems can also be helpful. Most cities have Bulimics Anonymous, Overeaters Anonymous, and outpatient groups from established treatment programs. At the end of the chapter, I'll make some suggestions

about finding a good therapist or for participating in an eating disorder support group.

I recommend that all women spend some time every day
thinking about their long- and short-term goals for themselves.
We live in a chaotic culture with constant demands on our time.
A few minutes a day alone can make a big difference in our lives.
With time to focus, analyze, and plan their experiences, women's
lives can become conscious acts instead of merely what happens
to them.

There are many good reasons to turn off the television.
Watching television reinforces the idea that what's important about a
woman is her appearance. Television watching is a sedentary activity
that encourages the consumption of junk food.

In therapy, on the streets, in offices, in grocery stores, and in
school meetings, women often look exhausted. Many women
report that they do not get enough sleep because they do not have
enough time. Many women's schedules need treatment. It's important to be able to say *no*. Women are exhaustible resources and
must take care of themselves. Women need time every day for play,
personal development, and relaxation. This isn't a luxury. Rather
it's a key part of staying mentally and physically fit. I encourage
women to write or keep a journal instead, because writing helps
clarify their thinking. I also encourage reading good books.

Almost every woman needs to work to view her body in a positive way. I tell my clients, "Your body is you and deserves your
respect and compassion." It's a good idea to remind yourself daily of
what you like about your body. A good way to do this is to stand in
front of a mirror and tell yourself what is pleasing. Thank your body
for being healthy and useful. Appreciate how fine it is in every way.
When you catch yourself being critical of your body, change the
subject. Tell yourself firmly to move on to another topic.

This new positive approach to bodies is tough to follow. In
America, the country that Paul Krassner referred to as the United
States of Advertising, we see bodies worshipped that are not like
ours. The Kinsey data showed that American women are more
negative about their bodies than women anywhere else in the

world. When Cassandra first tried to affirm her body, all she liked was her toenails. But after a time of hard work on controlling her thoughts, Cassandra accepted her body.

It's important for women to have faith in themselves. It's impossible for people to do anything that they can't even imagine doing. I encourage women to imagine themselves doing those things they want to do. Lie down in a quiet place and imagine yourself becoming a healthy eater. Imagine yourself exercising and loving the feel of your body moving and stretching. This exercise helped Gina develop an exercise program for the first time in her life. For weeks before she actually started to exercise, she visualized herself moving freely as she worked out. She enjoyed this image and later it helped her to do what she wanted to do.

Positive self-talk helps women stay optimistic. Many women keep a steady stream of put-downs running through their minds. This process can be so automatic that most women are almost unaware of their own negativism. This self-punishment keeps women from feeling hopeful and energetic. Positive self-talk means telling yourself what you like about your body, your personality, and your life. It means focusing on and reminding yourself of your strengths.

I ask women to write down three things each day that they feel proud of. Rose found this assignment particularly helpful. At first, she could think of nothing to feel proud about, but after weeks of searching for positives, she realized that she actually had a number of strengths. She liked her interest in music, then her love of books, and, finally, her sense of humor. Once she started to accept these positive aspects of her life, her depression began to lift.

It's important to view yourself as in control of your eating. To feel out of control is to be a victim, and victims can't make changes. Remind yourself that you can and will be in charge of your body. It helps to have positive fantasies of yourself in control. Carla imagined sitting down at Thanksgiving dinner and eating a plate of turkey and dressing. In her imagery, she stopped eating when she was full and moved happily and guiltlessly away from the table.

It's important to be realistic about yourself. Most women are not raving beauties. It's good to accept yourself exactly as you are. Many women feel that they would like their bodies if they weighed 10 pounds less. Why wait to like yourself? Do your best to like and accept your body as it is now.

Stop waiting to be thin to live. Buy attractive clothes now. Go to the beach today. Enroll in college or apply for a good job. Too many women put their lives on hold until they lose 10 pounds. Don't wait any longer to do what matters to you.

There may be times when you lose control of your eating, when you eat too much, or eat to sedate yourself. When you fail, try not to punish yourself. Most women with weight or food problems expect perfection from themselves. When they experience their inevitable failures, they are harsh critics. This harshness sets them up to abuse food again. Give yourself permission to make mistakes.

Closely related to perfectionism is a tendency to view the world in black-and-white, all-or-nothing terms. Many women feel that unless they are perfect, they are abject failures. In fact, most women experience a good deal of success *and* failure every day. It's best to have moderate expectations of ourselves. Early in her treatment, Cassandra suffered from this all-or-nothing thinking. She would wake up planning on being perfect in her appearance and her eating. Generally, she'd fail to be perfect sometime before noon. Then she'd tell herself that since she'd already failed for the day, she might as well abandon any efforts until the next day. A small problem would immediately lead her to a disastrous day. I instructed her to make several small mistakes every day. Also, as she left, I would tell her to remember, "The next hour is a new hour."

The longer I work with women the more convinced I am that women are too hard on themselves. Most women criticize themselves more than anyone else does. Many are all too good at feeling responsible and guilty. Following is a list of thoughts commonly shared by women with weight problems. My guess is some of them will be yours:

— I need to be good at everything.
— I should never make a mistake.

— I'm a helpless victim of my weight.
— Only criticism is true. Praise about me is phony.
— Other people are more important than I am.
— I must earn my happiness. I don't deserve it.
— If I avoid my problems, they will go away.

If any of these fit you, I would recommend a wonderful book—
I Can, I Can, If I Want To by Arnold Lazarus and Allen Fay. This
self-help book is designed to help women stop thinking along these
lines. I'm convinced that such self-critical thinking keeps women
depressed.

My first recommendation to women who come to see me
about their weight or eating is that they stop dieting immediately.
Diets *cause* obesity as well as eating disorders, depression, irritability, and sluggishness. A 1994 review found that the billion-dollar-a-
year dieting industry has alarming relapse rates. I recommend
throwing out your diet books, and getting rid of your calorie counters and bathroom scales.

As soon as possible, develop an exercise program for yourself.
There are many good books to help you decide what exercise program would be best for you. Make sure it's not too strenuous or
demanding in terms of time, skill, or money. Most important, make
sure you enjoy it. You are much more likely to keep doing something that is pleasurable. Walking is wonderful exercise and can be
combined with talking to a friend or enjoying the natural world.

Exercise feels good and contributes to mental and physical
health. Yet, I have seen women turn exercise into one more way to
feel badly about themselves. Some women become compulsive
and perfectionist about exercise. Others complain they don't look
good in their exercise clothes and feel heavy and unattractive in
their aerobics classes. These women are approaching exercise with
the goal of improving their external appearance. With these goals,
many are disappointed. But if you think of exercising as a way to
learn to enjoy your body and improve your health, as something
you do to feel good, then you are bound to succeed.

It's important to structure your eating in a way that comes
naturally to you. Avoid becoming too hungry, as this leads to

binges; avoid becoming too full, as this leads to attacks of despair and self-loathing. Have snacks available at all times. Women with eating disorders need to eat small, nutritious snacks many times a day to avoid bingeing.

If years of dieting have left you ignorant of your internal cues, you may need to relearn how to tell when you are hungry or full. Before you eat, think, "Am I hungry?" If the answer is yes, then ask yourself, "What would taste good to me and be good for my body?" Respect your own answer. If the answer to "Am I hungry?" is no, think about how else you might be feeling—bored, lonely, rejected, tired, or angry? Women are especially good at disguising anger as hunger. Once you have identified your true feeling, find a positive way to deal with that feeling. For example, for years Gina came home from work and headed straight for the refrigerator. She crammed food down her throat and later she'd be too full and guilty to enjoy dinner. Then one day, she slowed down and thought, "Am I hungry?" Her answer was, "No, I'm tired." She took a nap and woke feeling refreshed and ready for dinner and a relaxed evening.

Take a mini-vacation every day. Stop working for a bit and enjoy yourself. Be spontaneous. Be nurturing to yourself. Many women are driven workhorses who do not know how to slow down. Slowing down for a few minutes can make a crowded, hectic day seem special. I remember how pleased Corinna was with this assignment. For the first time in her life, she actually stopped and looked at some flowers blooming on her way to work. She said to me, "I'd never realized how beautiful and fragile they were."

We psychologists know that it is much easier to replace a behavior than to eliminate it. Substitute a walk after work in place of a snack. Knit while watching television instead of eating popcorn. It's important to break bad habits one at a time. Take small steps and do not give up. Record your victories over bad habits. Pay careful attention to what really works for you in fighting your addictions.

Everyone needs adaptive ways of dealing with stress. We can deal with stress in self-destructive ways such as eating or drinking too much, or we can develop some positive habits. Positive habits—such as exercise, reading, hobbies, or talking to a supportive friend—are nondestructive ways of regularly dealing with stress. Different things work for different people. Yoga bores me, but my good friend Sandra loves it. Cassandra resumed her painting, while Corinna joined a bowling league. Find what works for you. This may take a bit of time, but it will be worth it. Fortunately, once you acquire a positive habit, you will keep it. Good habits are as hard to break as bad ones.

After years of treating women with eating disorders, I felt as though there were *no* women who had truly healthy attitudes toward their bodies. Fortunately, I have met a few women who do love and accept their bodies. I want to write about one such woman so that you have a sense of what healthy looks like. We can learn from good examples. I've chosen my friend Brenda.

Brenda

Brenda and her husband Dick own a small dairy that they operate from their home a few miles from Lincoln, Nebraska. Brenda does the books and helps with the actual dairy work. She does most of the chauffeuring and child care for the two children in the family. Lizzie is seven and Toby is nine. They ride a bus into school and help with chores in the mornings and after school. Brenda helps both kids with piano lessons, and she coaches Toby's softball team during the summers. Like most working mothers, Brenda is busy, but she has managed to make time in each day for herself. Also, she's been thoughtful about exercise, diet, and stress management. She gets what she wants for herself and she knows what to want.

Her main time alone is during the mornings right after the kids leave for school. Before that she's busy with them and the dairy. But around 8:30 A.M. she takes an hour for herself. She writes in her journal and then jogs for three miles. That gets her heart rate up and gives her a chance to enjoy the morning. Often on these jogs she enjoys bird songs or sees a deer. She also thinks about her day and plans her time.

Brenda is careful about what she agrees to do. She allows each child to have two activities besides school. Sunday is family day, and no one schedules anything except with the family. Before Brenda adds any new activity to her life she takes out an old one. She does not agree to help with any major projects without sleeping on the decision and examining her time and priorities. She sees time, not money, as her most valuable resource and she is watchful of how it is spent.

Brenda and Dick are not wealthy, but fortunately what they enjoy most doesn't cost much money. They like friends, camping, picnics, fishing, and trips to see the sand cranes. Brenda enjoys watching a sunset more than she likes shopping or a fancy meal. Brenda's main hobby is reading and she checks books out of the library, so her hobby is free.

She has developed several good ways to cope with stress. Besides jogging and writing in her journal, Brenda has several close friends—including Dick—who she can talk to when she's upset. She and Dick have lunch together every day and discuss their lives and the children's lives. At night, they'll often sit on their front porch and look west as a storm rolls across the prairie or walk outside for one last look at the stars. Brenda has two close women friends whom she tries to see weekly and calls often. She tells these friends how she is really feeling. They laugh and cry with her.

Occasionally Brenda, who wears a size 14 and weighs 150 pounds, will wish she were thinner. She's gained 20 pounds since she and Dick got married. But she rarely thinks about her appearance. It's not what's important to her about herself. She's lucky to be married to a man who doesn't focus on appearances and who values her for other things besides her attractiveness. Brenda has never counted calories or been on a diet. She eats when she's hungry and stops when she is full. She loves good food, but doesn't think about food all the time.

Her father has a heart condition and Brenda counts the grams of fat in her cooking and uses the salt shaker sparingly. She does most of her own cooking, and fixes mostly vegetable soups and homemade breads. She is a semi-vegetarian—she doesn't always serve meat at meals and hasn't had a steak in years. She doesn't buy junk food or sugary cereals for the kids. But she isn't obsessed with avoiding sugar either. Occasionally the family will drive into town for hot fudge sundaes at the Dairy Queen. When she does have dessert, she doesn't feel guilty. She loves to bake everyone in the family his or her favorite cake on birthdays.

Brenda is lucky to be self-employed, which gives her more control over her schedule. But mainly her attitudes and behaviors are the result of thinking and working over the years to make her life healthy and whole. She tries to spend her time in ways that match her priorities. She avoids getting caught up in too many activities. She doesn't subscribe to magazines that preach the importance of being beautiful.

She's careful not to want expensive clothes or products. If she needed more consumer goods, she would have to work harder and she values the time with her children, her husband, her friends, and herself. Brenda, like most of us, likes to look her best and to feel attractive. But that is only a small part of who she is and it's not the most important part.

Brenda is a rare phenomenon, a woman who is relaxed about her body, eating and weight. It's possible for every woman to become this way. It takes time, energy and patience with yourself. It requires you to screen out messages from others. But with effort, you can be a person who fully accepts your own body and loves yourself for who you truly are.

Advice on Finding a Good Therapist

1. Get a recommendation from someone who knows your local mental health community. It's not a good idea to find a therapist through the phone book.

2. Call and interview therapists. Ask them about their professional experiences with eating disorders.

3. At your first session, discuss attitudes and values with your therapist. Make sure the therapist is nonlookist and nonjudgmental about heavy women.

4. Find a therapist who is well-read and who is aware of the role that culture plays in the lives of women.

5. Find a therapist who doesn't blame you or your family for the problems you are facing.

6. Look for a therapist who is smart, empathic, sensible, and caring.

7. Expect the therapist to have practical suggestions at each session.

8. Expect your therapist to be focused on solutions and to emphasize your strengths.

9. You should feel better when you leave most therapy sessions. Good therapists help you feel strong and hopeful.

10. Expect the therapist to be someone you trust, respect, and feel comfortable talking to about your most intimate problems. If you do not feel this way, look for another therapist.

Suggestions for Support Groups

1. Keep your group size between three and nine members. Groups with more than nine people have a hard time actually discussing personal issues.

2. Agree that everything discussed in the group is confidential.

3. From time to time, invite in guest speakers on topics such as exercise, the treatment of eating disorders, and nutrition updates.

4. Have group members keep a record of their "victories" over eating problems and share these victories with the group.

5. Arrange for a "buddy" system so that group members can offer each other emergency support.

6. Keep a group list of ideas for fighting weight and eating problems in a "good ideas" book.

7. Encourage all group members to develop and implement a wellness program.

8. Bring in materials from the mass culture and discuss how they affect the women in the group.

9. As a group, do community work designed to raise public consciousness of food and weight issues and to make life easier for women with weight problems.

10. Boycott products that are advertised in a way that demeans large women.

CHAPTER THIRTEEN

Helping Our Children

The Johnsons

Maria and Ed came in to talk about their daughters, Caitlan (12) and Brittany (10). Both girls had developed troubling relationships to food and the parents wanted to consult me on managing the difficult situations they were encountering .

Maria and Ed were typical of many middle-class parents. Both of them worked, Ed as a contractor and Maria as an occupational therapist in a large rehabilitation institute. Ed spent long days on the job, facing constant crises and phone calls into the night. He made it home for a meal about twice a week. Maria usually managed to be home by 6:00, but often she was exhausted. She didn't feel like eating, let alone cooking. Besides she never knew if anyone would be there for a meal. Caitlan was often at dance classes, school, or a friend's place. Brittany was usually home, but by six she'd fixed herself a frozen pizza. Anyway, Brittany didn't like many healthy foods and preferred to eat in front of a television. On most days Maria fixed herself a meal in the microwave and later munched on cookies or ice cream to fill herself up.

Ed often ate sandwiches or tacos on the run. Sometimes he ate with clients or employees at a fast food place or a steak house. He knew his diet wasn't all that healthy and that his cholesterol was climbing, but he had little time to worry about nutrition. At home he devoured large bowls of cereal or soda crackers smeared with peanut butter. He smiled ruefully and said, "I'm not someone with gourmet taste."

The girls presented opposite problems. Caitlan was a size 3, short and thin for her age, about to drop off the height-weight charts. She was a bundle of energy who had no time for or interest in food. In fact, since she was a baby, her parents had worried about keeping her weight up. They had to coax her to sit down and eat. Now she was getting lots of compliments on her appearance. Other girls admired her thinness. Boys called constantly and followed her down the halls at her school. Her dance teacher praised her small, lean body.

Ed and Maria worried that Caitlan's natural tendencies to disregard food were being reinforced, and that she might become anorexic. She often displayed that perfectionist, driven streak that can lead to anorexia. Recently, Caitlan seemed obsessed with her weight. She weighed herself daily and knew the number of calories and grams of fat in everything. She commented on her friends' and neighbors' weight gains and losses. She hadn't yet started her period and her parents worried that, because her percentage of body fat was so low, perhaps Caitlan wouldn't start.

Brittany presented opposite problems. She was stocky, clumsy, and, as Ed put it, "the slug of the family." As a baby her first word was "cookie." Even as a toddler, she'd loved to talk about food and had a great memory for meals and restaurants. She was an introvert who liked to be home, preferably in her bedroom. All her hobbies were sedentary. She liked reading, watching television, and computers. And Brittany was a junk food junkie. Her pockets were stuffed with candy bar and potato chip wrappers. She liked food to accompany any activity.

Maria would no longer take Brittany along to the grocery store because she begged to buy everything with sugar in it. Maria brought home mostly healthy foods, but Brittany was an ace at creating unhealthy snacks. She could make "sandwiches" out of chocolate sauce and soda crackers, fry up French toast and smother it in syrup, or make peanut butter and jelly tortilla roll-ups.

Ed and Maria noticed that Brittany sometimes used food as "pain medication." If she was stressed, hurt, or angry, she headed for the refrigerator. They wondered if she was addicted to sugar because she would get so angry when they denied her sweets. They knew she'd been teased by some neighborhood boys and that it had devastated her. Mostly they worried that she was beginning a vicious cycle. Already she weighed almost twice as much as her sister. She was gaining weight, which isolated her from her peers, which kept her more sedentary and lonely, which encouraged her eating.

As I listed to these caring but busy parents, I reflected on the difficulties families have with issues about food. Many homes have no "cooks," no scheduled meals, and no time for regular exercise. Meanwhile, children everywhere are pelted with two contradictory messages. One is "Buy this fattening snack" and the other is "Thin children are the beautiful ones." The Johnsons had one daughter who was acting on the first message and one who was acting on the second.

I recommended a few beginning steps. First, I suggested they hold family meals at least three nights a week. The family could cook together, preparing simple but healthy meals, and then all sit down to eat and talk. Ed would have to rearrange his work schedule, Maria would have to stop for groceries, and the girls would have to commit more time to the family. But this change might help the family structure their eating in a more positive way.

I also recommended that the parents tell Brittany that she could have only fruit after school, and that they require her to exercise at least five times a week. Both parents also needed exercise and I suggested that this could be turned into a family project. I recommended that they cut back on Brittany's television watching and on Caitlan's fashion and teen magazines. Finally, I advised them to throw away their scales. Ed and Maria liked my suggestions, but said they'd be difficult to implement. I sympathized but encouraged them that their family's health was worth the effort. I asked them to come back in a week with their daughters. We would all work together on these problems.

What Should We Tell the Children?

When my niece was a baby, she was bald and husky and we joked that she looked like Winston Churchill. Many people mistook her for a boy. Enthusiastically, they would say, "He'll be a fine football player someday" or "What a big, burly guy he's going to be." When we explained that Cora was a girl, their attitude would change completely. People would turn red-faced and apologize. Often they would say something like, "She's such a pretty little thing, I don't know how I thought she was a boy." Cora was *not* a pretty little thing. She did look like she'd be a football player. But, it's not polite to consider little girls anything but pretty.

Most boys grow up learning that their bodies are useful. They are encouraged to develop their bodies for many purposes, including work, athletics, and good health, and they are complimented for what their bodies can do: "Bob is a good runner" or "Carl will be a heck of a football player someday."

While most boys grow up feeling good about their bodies, there are exceptions. Small, slender boys have a tough time of it. Often boys who aren't athletic suffer a great deal during their school years. However, the range of "acceptable" bodies is broader for boys, and more tied to function. A large boy can feel lucky on the football field or a stocky boy can excel at the shot put.

Our girls, on the other hand, hear a hundred times a day that their appearance is what matters most. If we want them to believe otherwise, we must work to counteract our culture's lookist propaganda. Starting when they're newborns, we need to let girls know that we value other things besides their physical appearance. Most of us, with the best of intentions, make remarks that begin the process of the girl's later obsession with the way she looks. "She's a doll," "What a looker," and "Isn't she beautiful?" are innocent on the surface, but they suggest that a daughter's value is purely physical.

One positive approach to take with daughters is to comment more on function and less on form. For example, "Josie is an alert little girl" or "Patty has a good strong cry; maybe she'll be an opera singer." "Carrie is going to be a fast runner someday" or "Dixie is so graceful she would be a wonderful dancer." These comments teach that what is wonderful about a body is what it can do, not its status as an object to be evaluated.

We can also teach our daughters the joy of exercising. This will help them to view their bodies as sources of pleasure. Instead of thinking of how they look to others, they will think about how their bodies feel and perform. *They* will be in charge of the evaluation process.

Sometimes families perpetuate lookist values. It's not surprising. We are all influenced by our lookist culture. I can't write this without thinking of my chubby cousin Martha who lives in Rhode

Island. Now in her late thirties, Martha's weight has been her most discussed attribute since she was about eight years old. Recently my aunt returned from a reunion in Rhode Island, and I asked about Martha. She said, "Oh, Martha looks very nice now. If she could just lose 20 pounds more she'd be a knockout." Why, I ask myself, does it matter if Martha's a knockout? She's a married accountant. I'm interested in her job, her husband and children, and her hobbies. What books does she read? What music does she enjoy? But the only information I was able to acquire is how much Martha weighed this year.

It's so easy for our prejudices against the obese to rear their ugly heads and influence our children. Some people are blatant, "How can Sally stand to live looking like that?" or "If I weighed as much as Betty I'd never go out." But even the most well-meaning people often have subtle and pernicious prejudices. Even compliments about another's weight loss can be harmful, because they encourage dieting and anxiety about regaining the weight.

As a parent, one place I have slipped is in putting myself down for my weight. I'll comment on how chubby I look in a swimsuit and then I'll realize that this teaches my daughter to do the same thing. Children learn from the prejudices of others and may need deprogramming. For example, one high school student in our neighborhood thought chubby kids should lose weight so they wouldn't be picked on. He continued self-righteously, "It's their own fault. They just shouldn't eat so much." This was from a skinny kid whose mother reports he eats a half-gallon of ice cream at a sitting!

The messages children get from television can be very confusing. Recently, Sara and I discussed two commercials shown together. The first advertised shape-up outfits for little girls from size 6 on up. Girls could, like their mothers, dress for exercise classes. The shape-up suit ad was followed immediately by two candy bar commercials and a pizza ad. We talked about how hard it was for girls to want to be skinny and also to buy candy bars.

Obese women are treated in simplistic and stereotyped ways by the media. I have discussed with our children such questions as, "Why aren't heavy women the stars of shows?" or "Who gets to decide what kind of women are considered beautiful?" or "What other qualities do the women on TV have besides a perfect appearance?" Most important, "Are the people portrayed on TV anything like the people we know in our lives?" I have to laugh as I write this. I may have a tendency to overdo discussion. When I come into the room and the TV is on, my kids say, "Oh, no. Here's mom. We're in for another discussion!"

Keeping Healthy

One good strategy for helping your kids learn to eat healthy foods is to provide them with healthy choices. This eliminates power struggles while letting children choose what and how much they will eat. If kids have a choice between a banana and an orange, they will choose a healthy snack. Healthy and delicious foods should be served to company. This was really tough for our family. We went through a long period of transition when we ate sensibly most of the time, but when company came, we'd buy the chips, pop, ice cream, and cookies.

Ideally, food should not be used to punish or reward children. Many clients with eating problems remember that food was a reward when they were children. Grandma would say, "You've been such a good girl, I'll give you some homemade cookies." Or parents would punish children by not letting them have dessert.

It's good to teach children to give and receive affection in ways unrelated to food. Take the children for a walk after dinner rather than going out for ice cream. Watch a sunset together or help the children write a poem or build a kite. Stickers and hugs are good treats. I think one of the finest and most underrated gifts of all is simply listening. We all like to be listened to and feel really understood.

Ideally, our ways of celebrating holidays should become more personal, meaningful, and healthy. Halloween is a holiday that's been greatly exploited by sugar manufacturers. In fact, most of our holidays have become occasions for giving store-bought candy to kids. We need to develop more meaningful holiday rituals than gorging on expensive junk food.

We once had a baby-sitter who kept our kids entertained by bringing along an enormous bag of cheap candy. Our kids would sit and eat the candy while she called her friends and watched TV. Junk food is often the recourse of the exhausted or apathetic care-taker. It is a good pacifier. Tired parents are sometimes tempted to give children treats to keep them occupied. This may well teach children that food is a multi-purpose solution to problems. If you are bored, cranky, tired, anxious, or uncomfortable, eat.

We know that internally controlled eaters make the healthiest choices regarding food. We can encourage our children to stay internal regarding their decisions about food. We can ask, "Are you hungry or full?" It's probably harmful to encourage children to eat to be polite, to be a member of the clean-plate club, or to finish off something for us. We want to teach our children to pay attention to their stomachs and disregard the manipulations of outsiders, even us.

It's important to help our children learn to discriminate between hunger and their other internal states. Kids can confuse anxiety, boredom, loneliness, and anger with hunger. Well-meaning adults may further the confusion. "Oh, you look so tired. Come have some chocolate chip cookies." Brittany had a tendency to come into the kitchen when she was bored and say, "I'm hungry." I recommended that her parents encourage her to think a minute about how she really feels. Perhaps, she'll decide that she's not hungry.

Avoid putting kids on diets, as the externalization of control this encourages is hard to reverse. Regular exercise is a better way to keep children at their ideal weights—not to mention a great health habit that can help protect them from all sorts of food-related medical problems.

Teaching Your Children About Food

School teachers tell me that they have children who do not know the names of fruits and vegetables. Fourth graders who have been raised on microwave meals and junk foods do not know what a cucumber or pear is. In 1995, the American Health Foundation released a study documenting how ignorant children are about nutrition and how poor their basic health habits have become. Almost half the children surveyed (48 percent) thought apple juice had more fat than whole milk. One fourth of all children surveyed had eaten no fruit or vegetables the previous day.

It's important to teach your kids about healthy foods. We used the "red light, yellow light, green light" system. "Green light" foods are healthy, low in calories, and high in nutrition—for example, fresh fruits and vegetables. "Yellow light" foods are healthy but higher in calories—pasta, cheese, unsweetened cereals, and meat. "Red light" foods are junk foods like candy, ice cream, and potato chips. Children can learn to eat red light foods sparingly, yellow light foods daily, but in moderate amounts, and green light foods whenever they want.

Children can be taught that too much sugar, salt, and fat is harmful to them. They can learn to read labels and place foods in the appropriate categories. Our children have become experts at reading labels. Recently, Sara said, "It's amazing how many foods contain hydrogenated coconut oil." She is a cereal lover and knows exactly which cereals have sugar as the primary ingredient.

Children also need their parents to teach them to be skeptical about the messages they hear on television. Advertisers often associate their products with love, adventure, or happiness. Kids need to learn to see through these tricks. It's good training to ask them questions like, "Does Crispy Crunchy cereal really help kids have fun with their grandparents?" or "Do kids always laugh a lot when they drink Bubble Soda? Couldn't you have just as much fun drinking sun tea?"

It helped Sara to simply record a list of products advertised on Saturday morning. "Gee," she said. "TV is trying to get kids to eat candy at 7:30 in the morning." We've taught them that generally the cuter and more brightly packaged a product is, the less likely it is to be healthy.

Children need to know that not all adults care about their health, teeth, or complexions. Some adults care about making money, even when it harms children. Advertisers have developed arsenals of selling techniques they use to convince children to buy their products. We can help our children fight back by teaching them how to not be fooled by advertisers' empty promises.

Most importantly, we can make a tremendous difference in our children's relationship with food and eating by modeling healthy lifestyles. We can exercise, eat healthy foods, manage our stress properly, and not abuse chemicals. We can value ourselves and others for their character, personality, and intellect and not just for their appearance.

Tips for Parents

1. De-emphasize the importance of physical appearance in how you describe or evaluate yourself, your children, and others.

2. Don't turn eating and weight into moral issues. Do not use food as a reward or a punishment.

3. Insist that your children exercise at least five times a week. The best way to get them started is to set a good example.

4. Give your children the gift of your time, instead of sweets.

5. Don't put your children on diets. Do buy and serve healthy foods, and teach them about healthy eating habits.

6. Have family meals at least five nights a week. Everyone can help prepare the meal, which should be simple and nutritious. During these meals, turn off the television and do not answer the phone.

7. Plan family fun that isn't connected to eating. Most children love the outdoors and events that involve exercise, such as family roller-blading or hikes.

8. Limit your child's television viewing. TV promotes sedentary lifestyles, lookism, and junk foods.

9. Limit your children's exposure to magazines and other media that suggest that appearance is a person's most important quality. Discuss the media's stereotypes about the obese and the beautiful with your children.

10. Teach your children consumer skills, including a healthy skepticism about advertising.

CHAPTER FOURTEEN

Changing Our Culture

Margaret Mead defined an ideal culture as one in which there was a place for every human gift. This ideal culture would allow its members to grow to their fullest potentials, and would allow the culture the maximum use of its members' gifts. Nothing would be wasted.

But in reality, different cultures value and devalue different things. This leads to the expression and repression of certain aspects of personalities of the culture's members, and defines what is good, beautiful, and important within the culture.

For example, many African cultures valued cowry shells. Elaborate trade networks were established to pass these shells across the continent. A rich person was one with baskets of shells. Well into this century, the Chinese valued small feet in women. So young girls' bones were taped and crushed to make them marriageable. In pre-revolutionary France, elaborate hairstyles for women were highly valued. Rich women often had hair piled six feet high and filled with flowers, fruits, and birds nests. They were so top-heavy they could hardly move their heads, but they were considered beautiful.

Because of cultural patterning, different societies are vulnerable to different problems. A culture that values passivity will have fewer leaders. A culture that values aggression and guns will have more violent deaths. Our culture, because of its narrow definition of female beauty and because of the importance it places on beauty in assigning value to women, predisposes women to worry about their eating and weight and to develop eating disorders.

America is a land of individualists. We define most of our problems in terms of the failings of individuals. For example, even though the United States has the highest sexual assault rates in the world, sexual assault is treated as an individual's aberrant act. Individuals *are* responsible for their behavior, but cultural factors also contribute to the assault rate. These factors include our glorification of violence and our association of manhood with sexual aggressiveness. To fully understand this crime we must study both cultural patterns and individual cases.

In the same way, understanding food and eating issues depends on understanding how our culture affects our behavior. Living in America can be hazardous to our health. We are part of a culture of drug, alcohol, and nicotine users. We have the highest homicide rate in the world. Even our eating behavior has become disturbed and distorted. As a nation we should ask, "Why do so many of our young women have eating disorders? What has changed in America since the 1950s when the incidence of eating disorders was low?"

As a nation, we've experienced major demographic shifts since the 1950s. All over America, small towns and villages have disappeared. In the 1990s, most Americans no longer know their neighbors. We have many more transactions with strangers. This is a shift from what Kingsley Davis called primary relationships, in which people know each other in a variety of complex roles, to secondary relationships, where people know very little about one another.

Forty years ago Americans knew the people they met in stores and on the streets. Now we do not. And because we don't know anything about them, their families, or their history, we pay attention to the information that we do have—their appearance. This change makes appearance a much more important dimension of our relationships with other people than it was years ago. It's the only dimension we have for evaluating strangers.

Other things have changed. Advertising is both more intrusive and more sophisticated. When my grandmother died, we cleaned out her attic and looked at the ads from magazines of 40 years ago. They were laughable in their innocence and naïveté. In the grainy black and white photos the models looked like real people. A mother and daughter held up a plate of freshly baked cookies. A man stood proudly beside a lawnmower and his freshly cut grass.

No one was sexy or sophisticated. The ad copy concerned the product. Ads for slacks, for example, showed the slacks and emphasized the durability of the fabric. They make the jeans ads of today look like pornography.

Our lifestyles have changed. We've become a nation of couch potatoes. As a people, we exercise less. We ride in cars instead of walking and we do less physical labor. We are less physically fit than people were 40 years ago. But ironically, more of us have dieted. The March 1990 issue of *Teaching and Learning* magazine reported that preteens as young as 5 are preoccupied with dieting. The major worry of 8- to 13-year-old girls is their weight. By sixth grade, 79 percent of all girls want to be thinner than they are, and 59 percent have dieted. By age 13, 80 percent of all girls have dieted. On any given day in America, 56 percent of our women are on a diet.

I do not remember my mother and my aunts worrying about their weight. My grandmothers gained weight with age but they expected to do this. It wasn't a terrible problem for them, because gaining weight with age was seen as natural. The women in my family saw their bodies as they were, and they were content. Today, 90 percent of all women overestimate their own body size. The average woman feels fat, guilty, and responsible for her weight. She has tried and failed to lose weight and feels ashamed of her failure.

What are some ways of working toward a culture that is less punishing of women? We would all benefit from having a less look-ist culture. Just as we now have good programs that combat racism and avoid cultural and racial stereotypes, we could develop programs to counter lookism.

I remember the pride I felt when my son described a black friend who I was to pick up after school without referring to his race. He said, "Toby is tall, wears a letter jacket, and wears a blue Royals baseball cap." Few white people of my generation could do that. We tend to include race in our descriptions of our acquaintances. But for some children in my son's generation, race has become an insignificant dimension. I hope someday we can say this about weight as well.

Cultural stereotypes about the obese could be discussed and rejected. Children need to be taught that obesity is not a character defect and that all types of bodies are worthy of respect. The old saying that beauty is only skin deep should be dusted off and recycled for this new generation.

We can work to eliminate job discrimination based on appearance. Just as it's against the law to discriminate on the basis of age, sex, or race, it should be illegal to discriminate based on appearance. The ability to do the job, not appearance, should be the only consideration. Vigorous enforcement of civil rights in this area would help large women find employment fitting their skills. For example, women shouldn't lose their jobs in broadcasting when they are no longer young. We need women on television who represent all ages and body types. We need women who look like us.

We can encourage media—television, magazines, movies, and newspapers—to examine the messages they send regarding women and weight. For example, women's magazines bombard women with recipes for sugary desserts between their pictures of anorexic models. Cigarette ads often picture slim and beautiful women. Slimness, power, and modernity are associated with deadly products. We can write letters of protest to these magazines and boycott products that are not healthy. We can vote with our pocketbooks.

Free enterprise has run amok in the marketing of junk foods to children. Where is the responsibility that comes with the freedom? I'd like companies that manufacture and push unhealthy foods at our children blacklisted by consumer and child advocacy groups. I'd like responsible companies that market healthy products to get our support. It would be great to have more healthy options for our children.

Grocers who display junk foods in prominent places could be visited by local child advocacy groups and asked to keep the candy and gum away from the checkout areas. Some stores have started to have candy-free checkout lanes for mothers and fathers who want to try to keep sugar out of their children's diets. Let's support those grocers whose display of goods suggests that they care about our children.

We need public service ads on TV to counteract the powerful messages sent by advertisers. Through public service announcements, children can be taught to evaluate the nutritional values of foods. We need our children to see demonstrations of good dental hygiene and healthy lifestyles. Let's teach our kids to be good consumers and to love and care for their bodies properly. Let's make use of TV's powerful nature to beam out messages that will help kids grow up healthy and proud of their bodies.

We also need more public education on the pitfalls and dangers of dieting and the early warning signs for eating disorders. We can help these girls evaluate the media messages they encounter. We can teach them to resist messages that proclaim that their appearance is their most important quality. We can talk about the pressures they experience to be thin. This education should target girls in elementary and junior high schools, who are the most vulnerable to developing serious troubles with their eating. Prevention is more humane and less costly than treatment.

Historically, doctors have been more a part of the problem than of the solution. At best, they have supported women's beliefs that something is wrong with their bodies; and they've encouraged them to diet. And they have contributed to women's despair by their hostile attitudes toward the obese.

Doctors need more training about eating disorders. Girls who have raging disorders often go undiagnosed by their family physicians. Pregnant women with eating disorders do not get the monitoring they need. Women turn to their doctors for help, only to find that the doctors don't know how to help. Medical schools need to devote more time to nutrition. The average doctor studies nutrition for three days during medical school. This inadequate training does not qualify most doctors to give good advice to women. Doctors also need to understand recent research on the problems associated with dieting. Well-educated physicians could make a tremendous difference in our battle against eating disorders.

We should both promote and participate in wellness programs that stress caring for our physical, psychological, and social needs. By now, there are many fine wellness programs that emphasize regular aerobic exercise, stress management, proper sleep, and a nutritious diet. School children can benefit from developing wellness programs for themselves. They particularly need help with their stress management skills. Unless we teach them positive ways to cope with stress, they are vulnerable to the many negative options our culture offers.

Every town and city in our country needs support groups for the victims of bulimia and anorexia. Support groups have worked well in dealing with alcoholism—they should be free, accessible to everyone, and meet at a time when working women can attend. Women who have recovered have so much to give to those who are still struggling.

We have the tools to change ourselves and our culture, but we have a big job ahead of us. Teachers, businesspeople, doctors, entertainers, writers, parents, and mental health professionals can contribute to changing attitudes about women and their bodies. We can work together to create a society that has a place for every human gift. Just as bright and poor youth of whatever ethnic background should be able to partake of all that society offers, so too should heavy women be able to be whoever they want. No woman should be left out of public life because of her dress size. No girl should feel inferior because of her body. Let's work together to make eating disorders as antiquated as footbinding or exotic French hairstyles. Let's work to welcome all women into the sun.

Ways to Change the Culture

1. Work at reducing lookism in our schools, our homes, the media, and the workplace, through discussion and example.

2. Fight negative stereotypes of large people and encourage their participation in social events and public programs.

3. Encourage the national media to present diverse images of women, both by offering feedback directly to the media and by supporting media programs or enterprises that offer this diversity.

4. Teach yourself to—and encourage others to—evaluate bodies for their health and competency more than their beauty.

5. Prohibit the marketing of junk food to children who are too young to make informed decisions about their health. Support retailers who market responsibly.

6. Value children of both sexes for their characters, personalities, and intelligence.

7. Help educate children and adults on wellness programs, diets, and lookism.

8. Regulate the diet and food industries more carefully. We should insist on truth in advertising in both cases.

9. Discourage advertising that pictures bodies without heads, composite bodies, or photographically or electronically altered images of women. These unreal images increase women's discontentment with their real bodies.

10. Boycott products that advertise in ways that demean and hurt women.

Suggested Readings

Bepko, Claudia, and Krestan, Jo-Ann. *Too Good for Her Own Good.* HarperCollins, 1990.

Bruch, Hilde. *The Golden Cage.* Vintage, 1979.

Burns, David. *Feeling Good.* Signet Press, 1980.

Chernin, Kim. *The Hungry Self: Women, Eating and Identity.* Perennial, 1985.

———. *The Obsession: Reflections on the Tyranny of Slenderness.* Harper and Row, 1983.

Ellis, Albert. *Guide to Personal Happiness.* Hal Leighton, 1982.

Ellis, Albert, and Harper, Robert. *A New Guide to Rational Living.* Wilshire Books, 1975.

Freedman, Rita. *Beauty Bound.* Lexington, 1986.

Hanna, Sharon. *Person to Person.* Prentice Hall, 1991.

Lerner, Harriet Goldhor. *Dance of Anger.* Perennial Library, 1985.

Levenkron, Steven. *Treating and Overcoming Anorexia Nervosa.* Warner, 1982.

Orbach, Susie. *Fat Is a Feminist Issue.* Berkely, 1984.

———. *Hunger Strike—The Anorectic's Struggle as a Metaphor for Our Age.* Norton, 1986.

Pope, Harrison, and Hudson, James. *New Hope for Binge Eaters.* Harper and Row, 1985.

Roth, Geneen. *Breaking Free from Compulsive Overeating.* Signet, 1986.

Schoenfielder, Lisa. *When Food Is Love: Exploring the Relationship between Eating and Intimacy.* Signet, 1992.

Schoenfielder, Lisa, and Wieser, Barb. *Shadow on a Tightrope.* Aunt Lute, 1983.

Welbourne, Jill, and Purgold, Joan. *The Eating Sickness.* Harvester, 1984.

Zerbe, Kathryn. *The Body Betrayed: Women, Eating Disorders and Treatment.* American Psychiatric Press, 1993.